MERCEDES-BENZ
SL

John Heilig

Motorbooks International

First published in 1997 by Motorbooks International Publishers & Wholesalers, 729 Prospect Avenue, PO Box 1, Osceola, WI 54020 USA

Motorbooks International books are also available at discounts in bulk quantity for industrial or sales-promotional use. For details write to Special Sales Manager at the Publisher s address

Library of Congress Cataloging-in-Publication Data Available

ISBN 0-7603-0328-2

On the front cover: The 280SL was number three in the second-generation line-up of cars. Powered by 170 horsepower 2.8-liter engine, it proved to be the most popular of the W113-platform SLs. *Dave Gooley*

On the frontispiece: The handsome interior of the 300SL coupe. *Dave Gooley*

On the title page: The first of the production SLs is now a coveted classic among sports car collectors.

On the back cover: Evolution of the SL breed. From the 300SL at the top to the 1997 SLK, these are some of Mercedes-Benz most memorable and sought-after cars. *MBNA*

Printed in Hong Kong

CONTENTS

ACKNOWLEDGMENTS

This book would not exist had it not been for a chance comment from one of the major contributors to my first book for Motorbooks International, Steve Rossi. When I first met Steve, he was director of public relations for Saab. He later moved to the number two spot at Chevrolet, where he provided me with some fascinating stories about Donald Healey, who Steve had known because of his interest in Triumph sports cars. Rossi is a very complex man, an engineer with eclectic automotive interests who is involved in the field of public relations.

Between the writing and the publishing of *Austin-Healey 100 & 3000*, Steve moved on to take the position of director of public relations at Mercedes-Benz of North America. His first comment to me after assuming his new position was, "When are we going to see a Sports Car Color History of the Mercedes-Benz SL cars?" The book you have in your hands is the answer to that question.

I saw my first 300SL in the late 1950s, and I fell in love with it. I had an MGA and thought it was great, but when I saw this outrageous car with its doors that opened up, not out, I was mesmerized. Little did I know that almost 40 years later I would have the opportunity to express that affection in words.

Of course, Rossi isn't the only one whose support contributed to this volume. My editor at Motorbooks International, Zack Miller, shepherded the concept to acceptance, then the manuscript to completion. When a series of problems conspired to almost kill the project in mid-writing, his kick in the pants was enough to inspire the final push. Frank Barrett, editor and publisher of *The Star*, cleared up a lot of errors in the manuscript, and I thank him.

Another major contributor is the author of the final chapter, which we all hope isn't the final chapter on the SL, but which may well be the most important chapter of this book. When I realized that it would be impossible for me to attend the SL's launch in Florence, Italy, Joyce Tucker made the "ultimate sacrifice" and traveled to the Tuscany region for the unveiling. Many people volunteered to replace me, but Joyce jumped right in, obtained a passport in near-record time, completely blew off the Olympics which were in her home town, and got the job done. My deepest thanks for all she has done to help this project. She interviewed many of the key players who were in Florence and even appears in some of the SLK photos. Joyce is also a visitor from a previous Motorbooks International effort of mine: Her MGB led off that chapter in *MG Sports Cars*. Will this shameless self-promotion never end?

Another important person in the creation of this volume is Dave Gooley, who is responsible for many of the photographs. While I like to think of myself as a good photographer, Dave is great. And he has a bazillion contacts in the California car community with beautiful cars to photograph. Dave, too, traveled to Italy on this project, although it wasn't his prime motivation.

During a several-week visit to the Continent, he photographed the 1996 Mille Miglia in which Stirling Moss drove a Carrera Panamericana 300SLR. Dave also visited several prominent European car museums, including the fine Daimler-Benz Museum in Stuttgart. Dave, too, was a major contributor to my earlier Austin-Healey and MG books.

Writing about cars and car companies that no longer exist can be relatively easy; all you have to do is look in the records, interview a few people who were involved, and try to write an interesting story. With a "living" company that has its main offices on the other side of the ocean, the equation is more complex. Without the complete cooperation of Dr. Wolfgang Riecke of Mercedes-Benz AG, we would not have had the interviews with design chief Bruno Sacco or the several people Joyce Tucker spoke with in Italy. Our thanks also go to Bruno Sacco for his time; Helmut Petri, a member of the Board of Management of MBAG responsible for car development; Jörg Prigl, SLK project manager; and Helmut Werner, president and CEO of MBAG.

Thanks also go to Stirling Moss for a gracious interview on his experiences with Mercedes-Benz racers and production cars. Stirling and I exchanged phone calls and faxes for about six weeks before he finally sat still long enough in Florida for a telephone interview. I still owe him dinner.

On this side of the Atlantic, I must thank Lois Anderson and Pat Molina of Steve Rossi's staff for their untiring efforts in seeking out historic photographs from the archives. Thanks, too, to Maryalice Ritzmann, manager of brand heritage and community affairs, for books and literature that helped swell my library.

In addition, I am grateful for the use of the *Automobile Quarterly* research library. My former employer made available their numerous books that were helpful in the quest for information.

We would like to thank the City of Allentown, Pennsylvania, for permission to photograph Gloria Taylor's car in a "No Parking" zone (it helps that her husband is a police chief), and East Penn Manufacturing President Delight Bridegam for allowing us to photograph Harold Jones' car in front of his building. Other car owners who were gracious enough to permit us to photograph their cars were: Thomas R. Boyd, Monty Collins, Charles R. Glassman, Jean Paul Guiral, Len Hern, Harold Jones, Charles Lobb, Siegfried Roller, Gloria Taylor, and Jim Vance.

Stuart Schorr, of the Washington, D.C., office of MBNA, supplied the SL500 for my road test, as well as moral support throughout the project.

But my strongest thanks and love go to my wife, Florence, our daughters, and their husbands and fiancée, for all their support and love as we traveled through a difficult period in our lives. Without these seven wonderful people that God has blessed me with, this book and every other thing I have done would not be worth anything. Thanks.

—*John Heilig*

IN THE BEGINNING

A miracle happened in 1952, a miracle of automotive design, that stretched the boundaries of technology and design farther than they had been stretched before. And with that stretching, one of the most respected names in the world of automobiles became one of the most unbeatable names in the world of auto racing.

The miracle was the creation of the Mercedes-Benz 300SL Gullwing Coupe, a car that would win virtually every race it entered (it finished second in its first race), would establish new goals for other manufacturers, would retire nearly undefeated, and would create a new design form that would still be imitated 40 years later. Note: Gullwing was a nickname, not the factory designation.

But Mercedes-Benz was a company accustomed to making miracles. From the very beginning in 1886, the men and companies that would become Mercedes-Benz established a reputation for innovation that would keep it in good stead for more than 100 years.

The early history of the automobile was written by the bikers and the tinkerers. It was a natural progression for bicycle manufacturers to seek a faster and better way to cover ground, and motorized bicycles seemed to be a good idea. Early automobile industry giants such as Henry Ford; the Pierces of Buffalo, New York; and the Duryea brothers began their careers behind handlebars, only to see their horizons expand with the automobile.

Among the tinkerers were David Buick, a plumber by trade; Ransom E. Olds; and a couple of Germans, Gottlieb Daimler and Karl Benz. Daimler and Benz, working independently, saw the future in the new internal combustion engine perfected by Nikolaus Otto and shown at the 1867 Paris Exhibition. Otto patented his four-stroke internal combustion engine in 1877, and the man responsible for running the factory that built the engines was none other than Gottlieb Daimler. His assistant was Wilhelm Maybach, whom he had met while working for an engineering company in Reutlingen in the late 1860s.

Ever the nomad, Daimler worked for several engineering companies. Among them was the Maschinebaugesellschaft in Karlsruhe, the same company that had employed one Karl Benz 10 years earlier (or Carl, if you prefer; he changed the spelling). In 1872, Daimler began working for the Otto and Langen company. Daimler remained with Otto for 10 years, but left because he realized that he and the founder were essentially competitors in the development of the internal combustion engine.

Daimler moved to Cannstatt and eventually convinced Maybach to join him in the workshops he built from a converted summer house on the property. Their first patentable design was for a lightweight, gasoline-fueled engine that could turn 750rpm, a high speed for the era.

Mercedes-Benz prewar cars like this 1929 SSK set the stage for the 300SL and other postwar high-performance models from the German manufacturer.

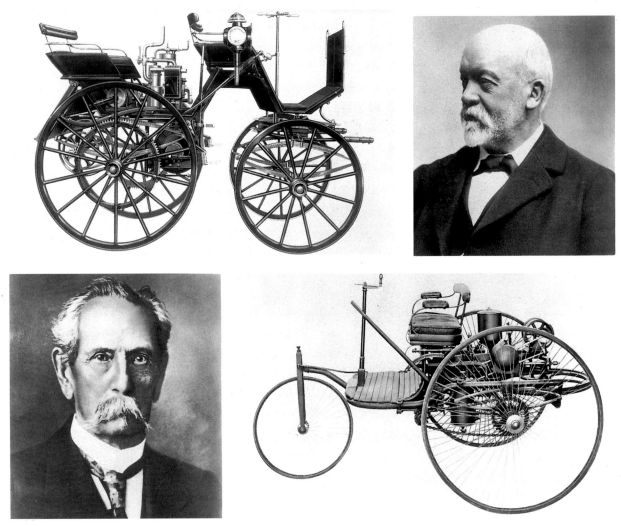

On January 29, 1886, the patent for the first automobile was awarded to Karl Benz of Mannheim, Germany, for his three-wheeled car. Gottlieb Daimler, working 60 miles away in Cannstatt, built the first four-wheeled car a few months later. Their companies merged in 1926 to form Daimler-Benz AG, manufacturers of Mercedes-Benz vehicles.

Karl Benz, born in 1844 in Karlsruhe, was equally obsessed, but he grew up poorer than Daimler. Benz's father died when Karl was young, and he was raised by his mother, who worked as a cook.

After attending high school and Polytechnic trade school, Benz began working for the Karlsruhe Maschinebaugesellschaft as a fitter. He worked there for 10 years, then set up a small company of his own with August Ritter. Despite financial troubles throughout the existence of this firm, Benz was able to develop and build his first two-stroke internal combustion engine.

This company eventually folded, but Benz received financial backing for the formation of a new company, Benz & Cie, which was created to design and build internal combustion engines. His plan was to use these engines to power self-propelled vehicles. Because Benz had been poor most of his life, he was not familiar with horse-drawn carriages. Consequently, his first "horseless carriage" was a brand-new design featuring a tubular frame, full-elliptic rear spring suspension, no front suspension, and only three wheels.

No one is exactly sure who was first on the road, Benz or Daimler. Benz *was* first to the patent office, though, with his 1886 Patent Wagen. His three-wheeler, with huge bicycle-like tires, a seat for two, and tiller steering used a four-cycle engine of his own design, although it was similar to the Otto engine. According to Beverly Rae Kimes, in *The Star and The Laurel*, "the

The hallmark of the early Daimler cars was a four-speed belt-drive system for transmitting power from the engine to the rear wheels. This feature allowed a smooth transition when changing speeds. Wilhelm Maybach is at the wheel of a Daimler belt-driven model that was built from 1892–1897, and Gottlieb Daimler is seated next to him.

first Benz [automobile] had three wheels because Karl Benz couldn't figure out how to steer a four-wheeler."

Daimler's first self-powered vehicle had one less wheel. In 1885, he put one of his small, sophisticated engines on a two-wheeler, thereby inventing the motorcycle. It would be the first and last Daimler motorcycle, but it would also be the first of many millions of motor vehicles to bear Daimler's name.

Shortly after constructing the motorcycle, a Wimpf carriage was located for the next step in the process. The Wimpf was a true carriage, designed to be pulled by horses. Daimler installed one of his engines in the four-wheeler and created a true "horseless carriage."

Daimler's car used a four-speed belt-drive system to transmit power to the rear wheels, making for a smooth transition between gears.

Meanwhile, demand for Benz's stationary engines was growing so rapidly that he moved to a larger factory. While Karl was busy perfecting the second model of his car, his wife Bertha and sons Richard and Eugen took the other "family car" for an extended trip to visit her mother 50 miles away. Except for the minor difficulty of having to push the Benz three-wheeler up hills, the trip was uneventful and successful.

Benz exhibited his vehicles at the 1888 Munich Engineering Exposition, even offering test drives. He won a gold medal.

Daimler's progress was equally impressive. Through a series of meetings that began at the Philadelphia Exposition of 1876, and culminated with a formal agreement in 1888, piano maker William Steinway of Long Island City, New York,

The brilliantly designed 1901, 35-horsepower Mercedes was a revolutionary achievement for its time. It was recognized by the motoring world as the beginning of a new "Mercedes era" in automotive engineering. The accuracy of this assessment was confirmed by the racing sucesses of the first Mercedes.

Barney Oldfield in the *Blitzen Benz* at Ormond-Daytona Beach, Florida, in 1910. The cigar-chomping Oldfield set a new land speed record of over 131 miles per hour in the car. Afterward he said, "The front wheels were shooting up and down in a weird dance, and I knew that if a tire burst I would be beyond mortal help."

became the Daimler agent in the United States. And while Steinway didn't see an immediate future for the automobile, he did see a future for Daimler's engines in boats and streetcars.

Daimler and Maybach were hard at work on an all-new vehicle for the 1889 Paris Exposition where Benz also exhibited. The wire-wheeled car used a two-cylinder engine and four-speed transmission, but it was viewed as a curiosity, not, as Pierre Giffard of *Le Petit Journal* wrote, ". . . the seed of a modern technological revolution."

Frenchman Emile Levassor was impressed with Daimler engines, though, and began production of them shortly after the Paris Exposition. He installed these engines in his Panhard & Levassor automobiles.

Emile Roger—a French automobile manufacturer and salesman—agreed at the show to buy an improved Benz automobile and become the French sales agent for Benz.

By 1892, Benz had completed a four-wheeler, which he called the Victoria. In 1893, he built the Velo, a compact version of the Victoria with a 1.5-horsepower, single-cylinder engine.

Although Daimler and Benz probably never met, the paths each took to automobile production were similar. Both, for example, believed in the value of competition. Two Benzes were entered in the Paris-Bordeaux-Paris race of 1895, generally regarded as the world's first automobile race. Hans Thum and Fritz Held drove the factory car to fifth place; Emile Roger finished 13th in a car sponsored by the French distributorship.

The *Chicago Times-Herald* race of Thanksgiving 1895, considered the first American auto race, also saw two Benzes entered; Oscar Mueller in the Mueller-Benz and Jerry O'Connor in the Macy-Benz. A Duryea won this event.

In 1897, Emil Jellinek purchased his first Daimler, a 6-horsepower, two-cylinder Double Phaeton. When he found this car, and his next Daimler, to be too slow, he ordered a four-cylinder 28-horsepower model. He actually ordered four, hoping to attract the attention of the factory. He did.

Jellinek used this car to compete in the 1899 Nice Week races. Among the events planned was a 128-mile race. Jellinek was entered under the pseudonym "Herr Mercedes," a moniker coined from his daughter's name. When his car proved faster than that of Baron Arthur de Rothschild's, Rothschild bought it. When Rothschild returned to Nice, Jellinek beat him again with his newer car. Rothschild bought it, too.

By the turn of the century, changes were coming fast in Daimler-Motoren-Gesellschaft, Benz & Cie,

Ralph DePalma won the 1914 running of the Vanderbilt Cup race at Santa Monica in his aging Grey Ghost Mercedes. He knew that a nonstop run was his only chance of winning. By mid-race, 11 of the 15 starters had retired. When DePalma tricked Barney Oldfield into making a pit stop, victory was his.

Rudi Caracciola in the Mercedes-Benz SSK, an unbeatable combination. With this model Caracciola won 26 events over two years. He is pictured here winning the Semmering hill climb in 1928.

On very short notice Mercedes-Benz developed the 1.5-liter W165 Grand Prix car specifically for one race: the 1939 Tripoli Grand Prix. Hermann Lang and Rudi Caracciola finished one-two and topped the previous race record by 13 miles per hour. After this race, the team used the 3.0-liter W154 Grand Prix car.

Rudi Caracciola (left) was the premier Mercedes-Benz race driver prior to World War II. He was able to win in almost any car under almost any circumstances. The Mercedes team, both prewar and postwar, was managed by Alfred Neubauer (right) who is credited with devising a system of pit board signals to communicate with his drivers.

and the automobile industry. Gottlieb Daimler died on March 6, 1900, "suffering during his final years and plagued by bitterness brought on by the restriction of his responsibilities," according to Dr. Fritz Nallinger.

Daimler also suffered its first racing fatality in 1900 when factory foreman Wilhelm Bauer crashed at La Turbie during Nice Week and died.

Jellinek offered to order 36 Daimlers with 35-horsepower engines if the factory would make him the exclusive sales agent for Austria-Hungary, France, Belgium, and the United States. Jellinek also wanted the models named after his daughter, Mercedes. The factory agreed, and the vehicle that was to be the first Mercedes was raced at Nice Week in March 1901. It won. "The new car simply dominated the week's events, winning the distance race, the sprint, and the hill climb," wrote Kimes. When Jellinek replaced the racer's two seats with a white, four-seater body, he also contributed to the creation of the first "real" car in history—a complete package, rather than just an assemblage of parts.

The fortunes of Karl Benz were not as great, however. Sales fell and competition from the new Mercedes model hurt his efforts. Karl's sons, Eugen and Richard, took control of the company, realizing that the simple little cars of their father would not carry the company to great heights. The vehicle that brought Benz into the modern era was the Parsifal, designed to be a direct competitor for the Mercedes. Introduced in 1903, the Parsifal was powered by a two-cylinder vertical engine and used shaft drive.

The Parsifal, although modern in design, wasn't particularly well-built. The sons left and Karl Benz returned to his company, albeit wiser. For the next 10 years, every new Benz had a four-cylinder engine, and these cars were designed for competition.

According to Richard M. Langworth, in *Mercedes-Benz: The First Hundred Years*, "Benz retained an official 'factory' driver, Fritz Erle. In 1907, Erle was joined by Victor Hemery, who had been chief of the research division for . . . Darracq for the previous six years. Racing fever swept the company rapidly. The 60-horsepower racing Benz of 1903 was succeeded by the 70- and 80-horsepower models in 1907, followed by a 120-horsepower racer in 1908. Naturally, all these cars still had chain drive." Two Benzes finished second and third in the 1908 French Grand Prix, while three Benzes took top honors in a reliability run from St. Petersburg to Moscow. Victor Hemery was the winner at a speed of 51.4 miles per hour.

Benz's last chain-drive car was its most powerful, and perhaps its most famous, the 200-horsepower *Blitzen Benz*, built in 1909 from a 1908 race car. The *Blitzen* (German for "lightning") *Benz* had a 12.5-liter four-cylinder engine that developed 120 horsepower. It was responsible for several records, including a distance record in a 426-mile race from St. Petersburg to Moscow.

The *Blitzen Benz* powered Barney Oldfield to fame, with a world record for the standing start mile set at the 1909 Indianapolis 500: 83.8 miles per hour.

The Mercedes-Knight

Mercedes was one of the many companies to use the Knight sleeve-valve engine in its automobiles. Patented in 1905 by Charles Y. Knight of Chicago, the Knight used a sliding sleeve, with ports cut into the cylinder walls to replace noisy valves. While this was an arrangement similar to that used by Nikolas Otto in his early engines, it was the first application of it in a modern engine.

Knight built his own chassis to carry the engine, "The Silent Knight," but achieved greater success marketing the design to other manufacturers and then collecting royalties.

From the first Knight-engined bodies built in 1910 until the last one built after World War I, the Mercedes-Knight proved to be reliable and quiet. A fifth-place finish in the 1912 Indianapolis 500 by Theodor Pilette in a Mercedes-Knight convinced John North Willys of the viability of the Knight sleeve valve, and he soon began production of his own Knight-engined car, the Willys-Knight.

Mercedes' chief supporter died an unfortunate death. Suspected of being a German spy because of his close ties with German companies, Emil Jellinek was imprisoned and died in prison in 1918.

On the road, Benz found its chief rival, Mercedes, to be building similar cars up to and into the early 1920s. The obvious difference was in the radiator, in an era where the "face" of the car was important in defining what followed behind. The Benz carried a flat face, while the Mercedes radiator featured a vee shape. All was to change in 1924, however.

The Companies Merge

In 1923, discussions began between Benz & Cie and Daimler-Motoren-Gesellschaft regarding a possible merger. While Germany had recovered from World War I, inflation had pushed the value of the mark to dangerously low levels and slowed automotive sales considerably.

On May 1, 1924, the boards of both companies signed an Agreement of Mutual Interest, which provided for a consolidation of the sales, promotion, and service departments of the separate companies.

One year later, an agreement to merge was reached. On June 28, 1926, the agreement was signed and a new company called Daimler-Benz Aktiengesellschaft (DBAG) was created. The insignia of the two companies were also merged. Daimler's three-pointed star represented Mercedes' past in aeronautics; Benz's laurel wreath represented its successes in competition. The combined insignia, a three-pointed star within a laurel wreath circle with the word "Mercedes" at the top and "Benz" at the bottom would last for more than 70 years.

Wilhelm Kissel of Benz became managing director of the merged companies. Among the engineers employed by the newly combined companies were future legends Ferdinand Porsche and young Fritz Nallinger from Mercedes and Hans Nibel from Benz. According to Kimes, "Doubtless Fritz Nallinger got his job because of nepotism, but he kept it because of talent."

Daimler-Benz Production Begins

The first two vehicles to carry the Mercedes-Benz star and laurel were named after the towns in which they were built: the Stuttgart and the Mannheim.

But it was in the field of auto racing where the Mercedes-Benz star (and laurel) would shine most brightly, and the man who would add luster to that shine was Rudolf Caracciola. In the first Grand Prix of Germany in 1926, Caracciola won in a Mercedes-Benz. Caracciola would go on to win hundreds of races in Mercedes cars before and after World War II, and he would carry Mercedes colors to Indianapolis as well.

Caracciola was born January 30, 1901, in Remagen, Germany, of German parents who had a trace of Italian blood in their ancestry. Mechanically inclined, he was apprenticed to a Fafnir sales agent in Dresden, where he soon began racing the company's cars.

His first win was in a four-cylinder Ego at Berlin Stadium. After obtaining a position with Mercedes-Benz, he convinced his employers to allow him to race in July 1926 when the regular drivers were in Spain, and it was time for the German Grand Prix. He won the inaugural edition of this event in a driving rainstorm and became a regular factory driver. While he raced for many manufacturers in his career, mainly as an independent, it was with Mercedes-Benz that he gained his greatest successes.

From the rather normal-looking Stuttgart and Mannheim models of 1926, the company introduced the Type K in 1926. In this case, "K" stood for *kurz* (German for "short") because the wheelbase had been reduced from 147.5 inches to 133.9 inches. The 6.2-liter six-cylinder engine was supercharged, raising the horsepower from the normally aspirated 100 to 140. The Type K had a top speed of only 90 miles per hour, but Caracciola won six races and hill climbs with one in 1926.

At the same time as the K was developed, Mercedes-Benz also developed the S, for Sports. Primarily a racer, these 180-horsepower, supercharged, six-cylinder cars could be bought by private customers. The SS was developed for owners who didn't want the S model's narrow body. The SS's bodyline was raised to make room for luxurious coachwork. The ultimate in this lineup was the SSK, which was produced in a short run of less than 50 cars. These spartan cars weighed about 3,700 pounds and were powered by engines that ranged up to 300 horsepower. Though intended primarily for racing, some customers had their SSK models fitted with custom sedan bodies for road-going use.

Mercedes-Benz K cars were the German Duesenbergs. They rode on outstanding chassis and wore beautiful coachwork, except that in the case of the Mercedes-Benz cars most of the coachwork was factory-designed and built. Initially offered with a 3.8-liter engine in road cars, this was soon replaced with a

5.0-liter straight eight in 1934. According to Dennis Adler in *Mercedes-Benz: 110 Years of Excellence*, the 500K could accelerate to 100 kilometers per hour (62 miles per hour) in 16.5 seconds, and to 80 miles per hour in 30.5 seconds. This from a car weighing over two tons.

The K's fully independent suspension was the work of Fritz Nallinger and Hans Nibel, and it featured a rear axle suspended by leaf springs.

In 1936, Mercedes-Benz installed a 5.4-liter engine in the K chassis, creating the 540K. This engine developed 115 horsepower under normal conditions and 180 horsepower when supercharged. The ultimate 540K was the Special Roadster introduced at the 1936 Berlin Auto Show and built to honor the 50th anniversary of the Benz Patent Motorwagen. The most expensive Mercedes-Benz up until that time, the 540K was painted silver, had leather upholstery, and a mother-of-pearl dash.

Rudi Caracciola in the all-conquering W125 Grand Prix car. The W125 won two races in 1936 and seven races in 1937. Caracciola led a one-two-three sweep in the Swiss Grand Prix in this car.

Like the 300SL that followed it, the 540K was produced in limited numbers; only 400 were built. The 540 was advertised as the fastest car in the world, just like its ancestor.

Described by Beverly Rae Kimes as a car that was "sporty as well as elegant and flashy without being gaudy," the 540K had panache and was a car for the few. It rode on a 129.5-inch wheelbase and weighed over 5,000 pounds. *Motor Sport* magazine described the car as capable of "a gliding crawl in absolute silence." The last chassis was built in 1939; the last car delivered in 1942.

The Glorious Thirties

Mercedes-Benz's racing successes continued during the 1930s. Under the direction of racing team manager Alfred Neubauer, Nibel's W25 won three Grands Prix in 1934 and eight in 1935. This 3.3-liter,

inline, eight-cylinder car achieved 354 horsepower on an exotic Esso fuel comprised of 86 percent methanol, 4.4 percent nitrobenzene, 8.8 percent acetone, and 0.8 percent ether. When the cars proved to be too heavy for the 750-kilogram formula, team manager Alfred Neubauer decided to strip the cars of their paint, leaving a bare aluminum surface. Neubauer's weight-cutting strategy gave the cars their nickname, "Silver Arrow," and would lead to all Mercedes-Benz racing cars being painted silver.

Manfred von Brauchitsch won the 1933 Eifel Race on the Nürburgring in a W25, and Luigi Fagioli won the Acerbo Trophy in Pescara and the Italian and Spanish Grands Prix. The Silver Arrows' main competition came from the Ferdinand Porsche-designed mid-engined Auto Unions.

The successor to the W25, the W125, won 7 of 11 contested Grand Prix races in 1937. Powered by a

PIONEERING SAFETY

After the war, Mercedes-Benz actively pursued the pioneering safety work begun by Béla Barényi in the 1930s. Barényi was a designer for Mercedes-Benz who had noticed in his youth that the center of the steering wheel of a Model T Ford formed a sharp point and was therefore a threat to the driver in a collision. He designed a low, wide steering wheel hub that was safer.

Barényi was born in Czechoslovakia in 1907 and graduated from Wiener Technikum in 1926. His school designs included a six-cylinder gasoline engine and a project he called "Future Volkswagen." After Porsche introduced his Volkswagen, lawsuits emerged. In a 1954 verdict, Barényi was credited with the invention of the Volkswagen concept before Porsche, re-establishing his honor as an inventor.

Barényi began work with Mercedes-Benz in 1939 after an interview with Wilhelm Haspel, in which he convinced Haspel that he could envision what the automobile would need 10 to 15 years into the future.

Barényi finally returned to his position as development engineer in 1948, following a long detention after the war. Production was picking up, and the future looked bright. One of his first designs was for a Terracruiser, where the driver sat in the middle of the front seat, protected from any side impacts.

His 1951 patent for a vehicle with a rigid passenger cell and deformable front and rear ends would revolutionize the automobile industry through the end of the century.

Mercedes-Benz began crash tests in 1959 in Sindelfingen under Barényi's direction. Results showed that in the event of a crash with a conventional vehicle at 50 kilometers per hour (31 miles per hour), occupant survival chances were zero. One of the prime reasons for this astounding number was that doors would fly open and passengers would be ejected from the cars. To keep the doors shut in an accident, Karl Wilfert patented the wedge-form door lock.

Barényi patented his safety steering wheel, with a large depression and deformable impact crown, in 1954. It was first installed in 1959 cars. In 1963 he patented his "safe steering shaft," which would not protrude into the passenger cell in the event of an accident.

Mercedes-Benz credits the philosophy developed by Barényi with its attention to the safety of its vehicles. For example, Mercedes was one of the first manufacturers to offer ABS and airbags in its vehicles. As we shall see later, in the present-generation SL sports cars, the addition of a roll bar that pops into position when the car's sensors detect a possible rollover situation, as well as windshield support pillars that are strong enough to support the vehicle, are direct results of pioneering work begun by Barényi's department. In the new SLK, door-mounted side airbags continue these safety innovations.

Because of his numerous safety innovations and more than 2,500 automotive patents, Béla Barényi was inducted into the Automotive Hall of Fame in Detroit in 1994.

1936 540K Cabriolet. Tested at Brooklands at 106 miles per hour, the 540K was the world's fastest production car of its time. It weighed more than 5,000 pounds and stretched over 10 1/2 feet between the wheel centers. Despite its weight and power, it was a relatively easy car to drive at low speeds.

5.7-liter, 646-horsepower, eight-cylinder engine, it was the most powerful racer of the prewar era. In this car, Dick Seaman finished second in the Vanderbilt Cup race at Roosevelt Raceway in 1937. Then followed wins at Monte Carlo, Bern, Livorno, and Masaryk. But the International Sporting Commission changed the racing formula at the end of 1937, reducing maximum engine size to 3.0 liters. Mercedes-Benz chose to build a 3.0-liter, 12-cylinder, supercharged engine for the 1938 season.

Manfred von Brauchitsch driving a Mercedes-Benz in the 1937 Grand Prix of Donington in England. His family had planned a military career for him, but a motorcycle accident scrapped those plans. He was one of Mercedes-Benz's most successful drivers prior to the war. After an unsuccessful attempt at returning to the track after the war, he emigrated to East Germany.

Mercedes-Benz and Auto Union received the largesse of the German government to aid their success against non-German teams through the era. The 3.0-liter W154 won six times in 1938, with Hermann Lang, Manfred von Brauchitsch, Seaman, and Caracciola winning successively. But Auto Union caught up at the end of the season, so engineer Rudolf Uhlenhaut cut weight from the cars.

In 1939, Hermann Lang won at the Nürburgring and the Belgian Grand Prix. A W154 piloted by won the Swiss Grand Prix and Lang won the European Championship on September 3, 1939, the day England declared war on Germany.

War and Peace

All Grand Prix racing and car production on both sides of the conflict ceased during World War II. Mercedes contributed to the German war effort and saw its factories nearly destroyed by Allied bombers.

When hostilities ceased, Mercedes-Benz returned as quickly as possible to the business of building automobiles. The company began slowly, building the 170, which was based on a prewar car. Daimler-Benz AG General Director Dr. Wilhelm Haspel saw his company build only some 200 vehicles in 1946, but production increased rapidly, and by 1950, more than 34,000 cars had been manufactured. Mercedes-Benz was back. In 1952, Mercedes-Benz returned to distribution in the United States as well.

Present Mercedes-Benz management attributes the success of the company after the war to seven basic principles: quality of product, Swabian [area of Germany] work ethic, plant location, product policy, Germany's rapid recovery after the war, a small group of owners, and the company's sporting image.

That sporting image was put to the test once the company had regained its momentum. The decision was made to return to competition. At first, the thought was to use a prewar car, or base a new car on a prewar design. But, as we shall see in the next chapter, that idea didn't work. After visiting Le Mans in 1951, Karl Kling, Alfred Neubauer, Hermann Lang, and Hans Herrmann decided that the best approach was to build a new car based on a production model. That car would be the 300SL.

DEVELOPMENT OF THE
300SL COMPETITION VERSIONS

By 1946, Mercedes-Benz had recovered from the ravages of World War II and was easing back into business. Just 214 cars rolled off the assembly lines that first year, but the number quickly rose to 1,045 cars in 1947, 5,116 cars in 1948, and 13,101 cars by 1949. The time had come for Mercedes-Benz to reconsider a return to racing.

But not without some classic conservative decision-making. How would such an entry be financed? What series would be contested? Who would be the drivers?

One question that didn't have to be pondered was who would head the team. Alfred Neubauer was the obvious choice based on his great prewar successes in that role.

As to the choice of vehicle, there was but one survivor from the prewar glory days, a 1939 W165 in the possession of another survivor, Rudi Caracciola. Shortly before the onset of hostilities, Caracciola had approached Wilhelm Kissel, then managing director of DBAG, and asked to take one of the 1.5-liter race cars and protect it so that it could be used when and if racing resumed. However, despite exhaustive efforts by Caracciola and Mercedes after the war, the cars remained in Switzerland, where they had been stashed during the war, and could not be used. The development of competitive racing machinery since the era of the W165 had relegated the cars to uncompetitive status anyway.

Once the decision had been made to re-enter competition, Neubauer began politicking with the governing Commission Sportive Internationale (CSI) to gain whatever advantage Mercedes-Benz could. For example, he tried to get the engine displacement limit changed to one that would give Mercedes-Benz engines a chance. He was unsuccessful.

Neubauer had watched Juan Manuel Fangio at the Swiss Grand Prix in 1951, and he returned from that event convinced that the affable Argentinian was the driver to head the renewed Mercedes-Benz effort.

With the new, postwar displacement limit for supercharged Grand Prix cars set at 1.5 liters, consideration was given to reviving the W165 racing cars. But after the 1951 German Grand Prix, which was won by Alberto Ascari in a normally aspirated 4.5-liter Ferrari, Mercedes-Benz decided that a copy of the W165 could promise only equality—at best—with what was then racing, never superiority.

The decision was made to build a new car. But since proposed 1954 Grand Prix formulas were 750cc for supercharged cars and 2,500cc for normally aspirated cars, Mercedes-Benz decided to scrap development of a Grand Prix car and concentrate its efforts on designing a new sports car that would conform to that class' 3.0-liter limit.

In his book, *Speed Was My Life*, Neubauer wrote:

The Mercedes-Benz Museum in Stuttgart maintains an excellent collection of classic and historic Mercedes-Benz racers and keeps them in running condition. Among these cars is the Carrera Panamericana 300SL that Stirling Moss drove in the 1996 running of the Mille Miglia in Italy. While not the full-bore race it was in 1955 when Moss and Denis Jenkinson won the event, the Mille Miglia today is more of an exhibition run. However, when drivers like Moss get behind the wheel of a car like the 300SL, even an exhibition run can be exciting.

We needed at least a year to design and build a new car. It would not be ready before 1953. To spend millions of marks on a racing model that would last only one season was obviously out of the question. And yet to put our racing plans on ice until 1954 was also a depressing thought. I suddenly decided to go to Paris and try to have the formula [1.5 liters for cars with superchargers, 4.5 liters without] extended until 1954.

I employed all my not inconsiderable powers of persuasion, and finally succeeded, after a great deal of lobbying, in gaining admission to the decisive meeting of the Commission Sportive Internationale [CSI].

After pleading that Mercedes' re-entry into international motor racing would give it a new fillip, I failed . . . . But our chief designer, Dr. [Fritz] Nallinger, came unexpectedly to the rescue.

"How would it be if we developed a sports model out of our latest private car, the 300? We might then consider. . ."

He left his sentence unfinished, but I knew perfectly well what was in his mind: sports car racing.

The head of our research department, [Rudolf] Uhlenhaut, was just as enthusiastic as I was. For whole days and nights he brooded over blueprints and finally produced something completely new: an extremely light tubular space frame. The only difficulty was the doors. How were they to be built in?

Nallinger and Uhlenhaut found a novel solution: the driver entered by way of upward-opening gullwing doors.

I'm never likely to forget May 2, 1952, the day my second youth began, the day Mercedes-Benz returned to motor racing for the first time since 1939.

The Players and Their Goals

"Nallinger I knew, but I didn't have much to do with," Stirling Moss remembers of the principal players in the drama. "Neubauer I had a lot to do with, and Uhlenhaut, of course, designed the car. Rudi Uhlenhaut was very, very easy to get along with, a nice man. Obviously he spoke fluent English because his mother was English. He was a brilliant designer and also a pretty good driver. His times were nearly good enough to qualify for the team, but obviously they [Mercedes-Benz] wouldn't do that because he was too valuable as a designer."

The goal for Mercedes-Benz was victory at Le Mans, then, and now, the ultimate sports car racing venue. Jaguar had won in 1951 with its new C-Type,

A 1954 Mercedes-Benz 300S coupe can be fairly considered the uncle of the 300SL. Both shared the same engine, but the 300S was more conventionally styled. The old 300 died in 1961; the SL continued to 1963. Many consider this car to be one of the most beautiful ever built by Mercedes-Benz.

based on the XK120 sports car, but with a more aerodynamic body designed by Malcolm Sayer. Neubauer was at that race with drivers Karl Kling, Hans Herrmann, and Hermann Lang as observers. They reported back to Technical Director Nallinger and Chief Designer Franz Roller on what they had seen and the directions they felt Mercedes-Benz had to take to become successful at the French race.

Juan Manuel Fangio leads Stirling Moss in Mercedes-Benz racers at the 1955 Grand Prix of Buenos Aires. Alfred Neubauer recognized immediately that Juan Manuel Fangio (in front) was the best driver to lead the revived Mercedes-Benz racing effort. He wasn't so sure about Stirling Moss (following), until the younger driver, in a less powerful car surprised everyone by becoming fastest qualifier over the entire Mercedes-Benz team.

53769

A 1952 Mercedes-Benz 300SL. As introduced to the press, the 300SL had its own registration plates and "short" doors that only extended to the top of the fenderline. In later racing and production versions, the doors would extend farther down into the body. In the production car, the slab sides were styled with "eyebrows" over the wheel arches and a huge vent cut into the front fender to allow engine heat to escape. Even so, the 300SL coupe could be a warm car to drive.

The engine for the new sports car would come from a sedan, the 300, which had been introduced in Frankfurt in 1951. Nallinger and Uhlenhaut had designed the single-overhead-camshaft powerplant, which used a cast-iron block and aluminum head. In its basic form, the engine pushed a 6.4:1 compression ratio and developed 115 horsepower. Fuel was mixed with two downdraft Solex carburetors. In the 300S sports coupe, the compression ratio jumped to 7.5:1, and there were three carburetors pushing output to 147 horsepower. In racing form, the compression ratio rose *again* to 8.0:1. With three carburetors, dual fuel pumps, an altered camshaft that changed valve opening times, special lightweight pistons, and a modified cylinder head that eliminated extra spark plug holes and reduced the size of the scooped-out volume at the top of the cylinder, horsepower grew to 175.

The frame was the most special and critical portion of the new car. The designers chose a lattice of small-diameter steel tubes in a triangulated or space frame, similar to that in the Le Mans-winning C-Type. Other manufacturers who had used space frames were Aston Martin with a 1948 model and the 1950 DB2, and Cisitalia with its sports and sports racing cars. Despite its relative light weight, it was a strong chassis. It had deep sections along the side and surrounding the cockpit to carry the drive-train components. Even the engine was tilted 45 degrees to the right (facing the car) to offer a lower hoodline. The tilting of the engine gave the driver added footroom, but the passenger suffered. And while the intake side of the engine was on the "top," the spark plugs were on the bottom, which made changing them a chore.

23

In 1945, Professor Fritz Nallinger led a group of 150 German scientists and engineers helping the Franch develop an aircraft factory. He returned to Mercedes-Benz as technical director in 1948 and was chief engineer responsible for the development of the 300SL and 190SL.

When Mercedes-Benz built the 300SL Coupe for racing, the space frame chassis tubes that ran down the side of the car would not allow "normal" doors. Consequently, Mercedes engineers devised the "gullwing" doors, hinged at the center of the roof. Alfred Neubauer was concerned that this arrangement might not be allowed. When the cars appeared at the 1952 Mille Miglia, the doors were protested, but the cars were allowed to run. Apparently no one contemplated what might have happened if the car had flipped and the driver had to make a hasty exit.

Unfortunately, there were no provisions for doors. Front suspension was independent by conventional, unequal-length double wishbones, coil springs, and telescopic shock absorbers. The rear suspension was the same swing-axle setup as used in the 300 sedan. The rear half shafts were located by coil springs and telescopic shocks, which were mounted behind the axles rather than in front as on the sedan. Torsion bars used on the sedan were eliminated for the racer.

To ease entry for the start of the 1952 LeMans race, the doors of the 300SL were enlarged from what they had been at the Mille Miglia. The 300SLs finished first and second, making a decisive contribution to the car's legend. The fuel filler was through the right side of the rear window. The jack was inserted in the hole in the bottom of the rocker panel for tire changes. For this race, the six-cylinder engine developed 166 horsepower, which was relatively modest even by 1952 racing standards.

Mercedes decided on a coupe body for its racer, primarily to give them better aerodynamics on the long straights at Le Mans. The aerodynamic efficiency of the body, designed in 1951 or 1952, can be compared with modern cars. For fuel efficiency first and top speed second, modern cars are designed to slip through the air with little hindrance. A coefficient of drag (Cd) of 0.30 to 0.35 is considered very aerodynamically efficient. The early 300SL's Cd has been estimated at 0.25! The exterior design of the car is credited to Karl Wilfert in Sindelfingen. The problem, as noted earlier, was that with the deep, space-frame sections around the sides of the car, there was no location for conventional doors.

The solution was gullwing doors, in which not only the side, but the roof lifted up, pivoting near the centerline of the car, to permit entry and exit. When both doors were opened, it gave the appearance of a bird in flight, thus "gullwing." Apparently, no one questioned how a driver would exit the car if it was upside-down, and, fortunately, such a predicament was never tested. In the first racing cars, the doors only extended to the bottom of the windows, though on production cars they would extend farther down the side flanks.

The 300SL's (S for "sport" or "super"; L for *licht* or "light") 94.5-inch wheelbase was shortened from the 300 sedan and coupe. Overall length was 166 inches,

with a height of 49 inches and width of 70 inches. Curb weight was 1,930 pounds without fuel and oil, about 600 pounds of which was engine and 110 pounds frame. However, the goal had been almost 200 pounds lighter, 1,760 pounds, which made Neubauer question how successful his efforts would be with it.

Uhlenhaut was the first to test-drive the car at the end of 1951 at Hockenheim and on an autobahn stretch outside Stuttgart. He remembered that it took Mercedes-Benz about nine months to complete the 300SL.

Birth and Baptism

Mercedes-Benz introduced the 300SL to the press in March 1952. The first race was just two months away at the Mille Miglia in Italy, 1,000 of the most grueling racing miles ever invented. Three cars competed, though entry was almost denied because of the novel doors. Drivers for the three teams were Karl Kling and Hans Klenk, Hermann Lang and Erwin Gruppe, and Rudi Caracciola and a Herr Kurrle.

Lang crashed shortly after the start, and Kling quickly moved up to second place. At the halfway point, entering Rome, Kling still led but was passed by Giovanni Bracco in a Ferrari 250S before Bologna. Bracco won by four and a half minutes, handing the 300SL its first and only major defeat.

A 1952 Mercedes-Benz 300SL cutaway drawing. The triangulated space frame of the 300SL is obvious in this drawing. Also obvious is the fact that it is a purpose-built racer, with an engine tilted to allow a lower hoodline and twin spare tires for long-distance races where the driver might have to change his own flats along the route.

The next race for the cars was in a sports car supporting race before the Swiss Grand Prix in Berne. Four 300SL cars were entered, one for each of the three Mille Miglia drivers and Fritz Reiss. They were painted red, white, blue, and silver in recognition of Switzerland's neutrality. Kling won, followed by Lang and Reiss. Caracciola was in fourth place when he crashed into a tree, breaking his leg. He spent the remainder of 1952 in traction and later retired.

Le Mans was the prime goal of the 300SLs, and that race followed in mid-June. Four cars were again entered. Three ran, with the teams of Kling and Klenk, Lang and Reiss, and Theo Helfrich and Norbert Niedermeyer. One test car had an experimental air brake fitted to assist in slowing from the high speeds on the Mulsanne Straight, but it was not used in the race.

With all three examples of the previous year's champion, the Jaguar C-Type, out of the race in the first hour with overheating engines caused by a new front-end design, the race was open to all comers. With just over an hour to go in the race, Pierre Levegh had built up a four-lap lead in a solo effort, driving a

French Talbot. However, the intense strain caught up with him and a missed shift blew his engine.

Lang and Reiss inherited the win, followed by Helfrich and Niedermeyer in second place. Kling and Klenk drove the fastest car in the race, but retired early with generator failure.

Then it was home to the Nürburgring for the Le Mans-winning SLs in August for a sports car race that supported the German Grand Prix. Six cars appeared in practice: four roadsters and two coupes. The winner was Lang in a roadster ahead of Kling, Reiss, and Helfrich, also in roadsters.

The final race for 1952 was the Mexican Carrera Panamericana. Three cars were entered, coupes for Kling and Klenk, and Lang and Gruppe, and a roadster for American John Fitch and Eugen Geiger.

After protests were lodged by other teams, Fitch was disqualified for backing over the starting line after one stage in order to return to the service depot to have his car worked on. He continued as a "non-combatant" and set the fastest time on the final leg.

Lang had a problem during the next-to-last stage when his driver's door blew off, forcing him

Mercedes-Benz 1954 300SL-S streamlined racer was powered by a 3.0-liter, inline, eight-cylinder engine rated at 257 horsepower. The first time the car raced was at the French Grand Prix at Reims, where Juan Manuel Fangio and Karl Kling finished one-two. Fangio called the car "perfect" and said it was "the machine which every driver dreams of."

out of the race. Kling was the overall winner in the other 300SL, though, completing a near-perfect season for Mercedes-Benz's stunning new sports car.

Dominance then Retirement

After the 1952 season ended, Mercedes-Benz withdrew from sports car racing, to concentrate on GP racing. For the 1954 season, the company would compete in grand prix races under a new formula. It would return to sports car racing in 1955 in a car derived from the W196 GP car, the eight-cylinder 300SLR.

The 300SLR led Mercedes-Benz to its most successful, and tragic, year in racing. The car won the Mille Miglia with Stirling Moss driving and Denis Jenkinson as navigator, it won the ADAC Eifel Race, the Swedish Grand Prix, the Tourist Trophy, and the Targa Florio, and in the end the International Sports Car Championship.

In the Mille Miglia, Moss drove with abandon, following Jenkinson's carefully prepared route instructions

with complete faith. But Moss said later that the 300SLR Mille Miglia car wasn't particularly easy to drive. "It was a great car because it was reliable and no problem from that point of view," Moss said. "But it was a large car and felt quite big. It wasn't as nimble as other cars, but it was extremely strong. It was a bit difficult in the wet."

Moss drove the same car at Le Mans in 1955. "That car won all the world championship races we completed," Moss said. "And we certainly would have won Le Mans if we had finished, because we had a 20-minute lead when we pulled out."

The reason the car, and the entire Mercedes-Benz team, withdrew from the 1955 race was a disaster that occurred in the fourth hour and that resulted in the deaths of over 80 spectators and driver Pierre Levegh.

According to most observers of the accident, Lance Macklin was going down the pit straight in his Austin-Healey 100S when Mike Hawthorne passed him in his

A 1954 W196R streamlined racer, which used a modified 300SL-S space frame with an eight-cylinder engine installed. It won at the French Grand Prix in its first race, but finished fourth in its next outing at Silverstone. Fangio drove an open-wheel version for the rest of the season, winning in Germany, Switzerland, and Italy. Karl Kling retained the streamliner for the German Grand Prix.

D-Type Jaguar. After passing Macklin, Hawthorne braked and cut in front of the Healey to head for his pits. This action forced Macklin to take evasive action, which meant turning left. When he did this, Levegh, who was coming up behind in his Mercedes, struck the left rear of the Healey. The 300SLR catapulted into the air and into the crowd massed opposite the pits. With its magnesium components, the Mercedes burst into white-hot flames, killing 82 people and injuring more than 100.

Roger Menadue, who was responsible for developing and tuning the Austin-Healey Le Mans cars, told me that he thought Hawthorne misjudged the speed of the Healey. Menadue said: "I heard Mike Hawthorne say to Lance Macklin after the crash, 'I never realized you were going so fast, Lance.' I think poor Mike misjudged the speed. He thought there was an ordinary Healey out there which had a top speed of about 120.

"Instead of that there was this 100S out there— it was the first time it had ever appeared at Le Mans—

and that damned thing was going down the Mulsanne Straight at 150!"

After much discussion with Stuttgart through the night, the entire Mercedes-Benz team withdrew from the race as a gesture of respect for those who had died. Some reports said that the team would have withdrawn earlier, but the departing crowds might have hampered the rescue efforts.

Nevertheless, Moss wasn't pleased with the decision. "I think it was a wrong decision, really," he said recently. "Obviously, the fact that we were winning affected my thoughts. But I think it was the wrong decision because it wouldn't help with the problems of the disaster that happened. I think all it really did was make a few people think that because they pulled out maybe they had a little bit of guilt about it, which was entirely wrong. It was nothing to do with Mercedes causing of the accident. They happened to be involved, but it really wasn't Mercedes' fault."

John Fitch was the first American driver on the Mercedes-Benz team. Here he is seen in the Carrera Panamericana car in which he was disqualified for reversing over the starting line of one stage to return to the garage area for repairs. As a "non-combatant," he still set the fastest time in the final leg of the race.

Moss takes particular umbrage about comments by "some American idiot [who shall remain nameless] who had the absolutely ridiculous idea that Mercedes-Benz were running on nitromethane and that's why the car exploded."

On October 16, 1955, Neubauer had the pleasure of seeing his car win the Targa Florio at the hands of Peter Collins and Stirling Moss, as well as the sorrow of finding out that Mercedes-Benz would withdraw from racing again. In its two years of competition, the supremely dominant 300SL and 300SLR were unlike any other automobile. They proved to be the premier vehicle for the greatest drivers of their era: Juan Manuel Fangio and Stirling Moss. And of course, they created a legend.

After the Targa win, Neubauer, recounting his feelings in his autobiography, recalled:

That was certainly one of the happiest days in my life—till I got back to the villa where we were staying. There I found a letter waiting for me, marked "Personal and Confidential" and dated October 12, 1955. I opened it. It was from Professor Nallinger. As I read it, I felt as if

One of the Mercedes-Benz 300SLR's greatest triumphs was in the 1955 Mille Miglia. The car was driven by a young Stirling Moss (right), who followed the meticulous route notes prepared by co-driver and journalist Denis Jenkinson (second from left). In this picture, the victorious team is congratulated by Alfred Neubauer (center) and Rudi Uhlenhaut (left).

the bottom had dropped out of my world.

One sentence in that letter is still engraved in my memory. "The Board of Directors has decided, after the most careful considerations, to withdraw from motor racing for several years."

Six days later, at the traditional end-of-season ceremony at the works at Unterturkheim, Fangio and Kling, Stirling Moss and Peter Collins were told that Mercedes' racing days were over. So when the prizes had been distributed, the speeches made and the photographs taken, there came the farewells I had been dreading. It was the end of a great era.

Two 300SLR "Gullwing" coupe road cars were built, based on the eight-cylinder sports racer. The coupe was the official car of Rudi Uhlenhaut, and would have made an exceptionally beautiful successor to the 300SL had it entered production. A roadster version was never completed.

Mercedes-Benz had already begun series production of the road-going version of the 300SL Coupe when the company retired from racing in 1955. The production 300SL Roadster followed for model year 1957. Both of these cars would perpetuate the memory of the competition 300SLs and their amazing records.

Its grille is clean and ping-free now, but there was a time when this 300SLR Carrera Panamericana car was pock-marked with stone dents from the race through Mexico. Mercedes won the race, of course. In its time, the Panamericana was the equivalent of today s Baja 1000, except it was contested with racing and production cars rather than purpose-built off-road machinery. The first race was held in May 1950 and was won by Herschel McGriff and Ray Elliot in an Oldsmobile. Ferrari Vignale coupes took the top places in 1951. Lancia won in 1953 and Ferrari in 1954, the last year for the event. More than 20 drivers and spectators were killed during the five years of the Panamericana.

Stirling Moss continues to be a goodwill ambassador for Mercedes-Benz. He regularly competes in the Mille Miglia retrospective runs with a 300SL Panamericana coupe. This is a restored version of the car that competed in the 1953 Mexican road race. Moss won the 1955 Mille Miglia in a 300SLR roadster with Denis Jenkinson as navigator.

300SL "GULLWING" COUPE PRODUCTION CAR

Though a great era in Mercedes-Benz auto racing may have come to an end, it marked the beginning of a fantastic line of production cars. Once again, a visionary came to the rescue, this time in the form of U.S. Mercedes-Benz importer, Max Hoffman.

Hoffman had a magnificent Frank Lloyd Wright-designed showroom on Park Avenue in New York City with a spiral display ramp and a mirrored, three-cornered star in the ceiling. He also had an uncanny sense of what would sell. He knew the 300SL could be a popular car in Mercedes-Benz showrooms, particularly in the United States, and convinced the factory of that fact with a significant order.

Rudi Uhlenhaut remembered, "He guaranteed that he would buy a considerable number. . . . We hadn't expected that anybody would buy five hundred, but Hoffman was a very good businessman, and he saw the chance for this type of car in the American market. He ordered 1,000."

As Karl Ludvigsen wrote in *Automobile Quarterly*, volume 10, number 2:

> [Hoffman] was invited to present his case before the Daimler-Benz management committee. Its chairman, Fritz Koenecke, allowed Max to speak his piece and then invited comments from the other committee members. One of the first to respond was the engineering director,

Fritz Nallinger, who said that such a car should be built on the platform frame that was then being used for the 180 sedan. Almost instantly Hoffman spoke up: *"Das wird Nichts."* ("Nothing will come of that.")

A rustle of uneasiness circled the table at this open and frank challenge to the veteran Nallinger, who was then regarded as the uncrowned king of Daimler-Benz. "I didn't really think before I said it," Hoffman admits. Koenecke carried the meeting ahead smoothly, overlooking this indiscretion. Hoffman was given a chance for a more formal reply, in which he said that a modified sedan chassis would be too long and heavy for the power available. "But I lost," he remembers, "and the 190SL was the result."

Nevertheless, Max Hoffman had helped bring a Mercedes-Benz sports car to life. He emphasizes that it was the 190SL that was important to him, not the much more famous 300SL that was also developed into a production model with Max's encouragement. "Without the smaller car," Max says, "the 300SL would not have come along." In fact Hoffman, a lover of small, light, and pleasant sports cars, did not care for the 300SL.

"The Baron of Park Avenue," as Ludvigsen called Hoffman, was born in Vienna in 1904. His father had a general store, and eventually migrated into manufacturing sewing machines. The younger Hoffman began

---

While the racing version of the 300SL was an efficient and successful car, it was somewhat drab with its slab sides and lack of ornamentation. For the production version, features like the cooling vents, chrome flashes, "eyebrows," and cooling vents over the rear window, added character to the car and made it more attractive.

The production Mercedes-Benz 300SL was introduced at the 1954 New York Auto Show. On the stand with the car was a prototype 190SL with styling that never made it to the final production car in 1955.

competing in club races in 1920 on a DKW motorcycle (really more of a motorized bicycle). His first automobile was an Amilcar CS. In the 1930s, he owned a Citroën Traction Avant while he lived in Paris.

In the mid-1930s, Hoffman became the Middle European representative for Rolls-Royce, Bentley, Alfa Romeo, Talbot, Delahaye, Volvo, and Hotchkiss. He didn't represent Mercedes-Benz because he felt it was too heavy.

When Hoffman emigrated to the United States in 1941, he had little knowledge of the language or business procedures. When the United States entered the war, he dropped all automotive aspirations and began making plastic costume jewelry which he then had metalized.

By the end of the war, he was able to return to his first love, automobiles. Eventually he became the importer for H.R.G., Lea-Francis, Healey, Lagonda, Daimler (the British one), and Lanchester. He also began importing Jaguar, BMW, and the early Volkswagen.

In 1951, Hoffman began negotiations with Daimler-Benz AG to import Mercedes-Benz cars. Sir William Lyons, head of Jaguar, tried to dissuade Hoffman from importing the German cars because there were still some bitter feelings remaining from the war and because Lyons saw Mercedes as a

competitor. He wasn't successful. Hoffman set up a new company, Mercedes-Benz Distributors, Inc., to import the marque. Lyons' disapproval of Hoffman's move eventually led to Jaguar breaking relations with Hoffman in 1954.

Hoffman was instrumental in convincing Daimler-Benz to add lighter colors to the Mercedes line, and to create a production version of the 300SL, as well as a smaller sports car, the 190SL. Hoffman's relationship with Daimler-Benz ended in 1957 when he was bought out by Curtiss-Wright, which had a management contract with Studebaker-Packard. This led to the unlikely combination of Mercedes-Benz cars being sold in Studebaker dealerships. This halo effect didn't work for Studebaker, however, and the firm was out of business in a few years.

"If Hoffman hadn't been there, there wouldn't have been any production. But he knew what you could sell in America and he took the risk. 'I'll do it,' he said," recalled Rudi Uhlenhaut.

Introducing the 300SL . . . and 190SL

In March 1954, the production version of the 300SL was shown at the International Motor Sports Show in the Seventh Regiment Armory in New York. Next to it was a prototype of the 190SL, which went into production in 1955.

The production 300SL closely resembled the racing version, with subtle differences to make it more amenable for road-going drivers. "The now legendary 300SL "Gullwing" of 1954 can be classified as a virtuoso performance in a symphony of design!" wrote Daimler-Benz Director of Design Bruno Sacco in *Mercedes-Benz Design*. "The design and styling concept have a racing pedigree, and are only slightly 'civilized.' The true designers of the 300SL are to be found among the engineers who, in 1952, were able to put a successful racing car on the circuit.

"The step from this concept to the standard SL two years later was not very big, and yet remarkably successful. I think it is appropriate to mention its two designers: Rudolph Uhlenhaut, at that time the director of passenger car research and development, who designed the competition version, and Karl Wilfert, later the head of body engineering, who did the 'standard' model."

Racing experience was the source of many improvements for the production version of the car. For example, while the engine was still tilted 45 degrees to the right to create a lower hoodline, it was equipped with direct fuel injection, which helped create 215 horsepower and a maximum speed of 162 miles per hour with the

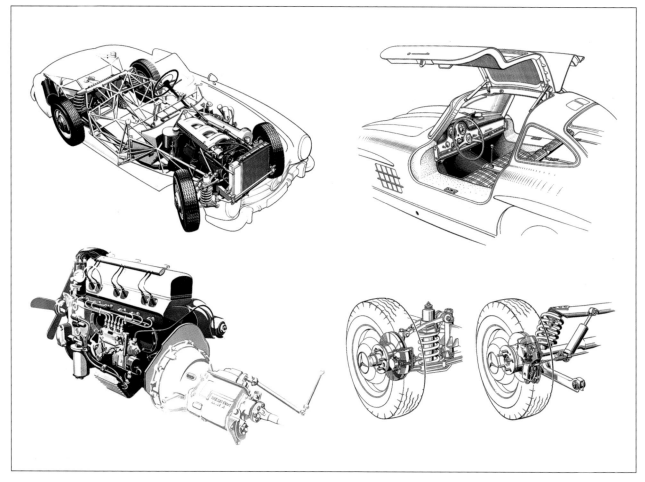

Drawings of the 300SL coupe body and components show the inner workings of the coupe. Early production versions were upholstered in the same plaid cloth, which seems incongruous. Few 300SL restorations retain the plaid cloth upholstery, with most owners preferring leather.

3.64:1 rear axle. Horsepower in the original racing version of the car was listed at as low as 190. In addition, the vacuum-drum brakes were finned for cooling but were otherwise identical to those used on the 300 sedan.

Fuel injection may have been an unusual choice for the period, but Daimler-Benz had experience with injected engines reaching back into the 1930s, and, of course, used it on airplane engines during the war.

Rudolf Uhlenhaut wrote: "From extensive use of [fuel] injection during the war Mercedes found that the system had the effect of upgrading the octane rating of the fuel. With racing fuels it then becomes possible to use higher compression ratios."

Fritz Nallinger added: "Modern racing engines are invariably high-revving and in the lower speed range are usually what is commonly

termed 'hollow.' Their best performance is reached above 50 percent to 70 percent of maximum revolutions, thus only giving high performance at a relatively high speed. In consequence of this consideration, it was to be expected that the four-stroke engine, with a wide speed range, could be made to maintain a more even range of power if the correct amount of [fuel] was injected into each cylinder at all speeds. More power at all speeds should be the result. [Fuel] Injection also promised more economical consumption figures."

While the doors retained the "gullwing" feature of the racing cars, they now extended about halfway down the side instead of ending just below the window frame, making for easier entry and exit. In addition, small wing windows were added for ventilation. It was still impossible for the windows to roll down into the door, so the glass was mounted in detachable

Modern car designers are concerned about the drag coefficient—how efficiently a car moves through the air. Using computer-aided-design techniques, modern cars are considered aerodynamic if they have a drag coefficient of 0.30 to 0.35. The designers of the 300SL, working intuitively and without the benefit of huge computers, achieved a drag coefficient with the 300SL coupe of 0.25, making it one of the most aerodynamic production cars of all time.

frames in the production cars. These could be lifted out and stored in special pockets behind the seats.

To a casual observer, the race car and production car were identical twins, but under closer inspection they were more like fraternal twins. Only the roof, rear end, and window shapes were the same.

The doors were redesigned and lengthened for easier entry. And the front of the doors was curved forward for a cleaner design. Spring-loaded struts propped them open.

Up front, the fenders were more pronounced, while the widened grille, with its center-mounted three-pointed

Because of the high doorsills caused by its space-frame construction, conventional doors could not be used on the racing version of the 300SL. Alfred Neubauer pored over the regulations prior to entry of the car in the 1953 Mille Miglia (its first race) and could find no rules outlawing upward-opening doors. Some teams protested, but the car was permitted to run, and a legend was born.

star, was more compatible with the rest of the front fascia. Though the racers could make do with a single headlight on each side, this wouldn't work for the production model which needed, in addition to headlights, turn signal indicators and chrome bumpers. In the Roadster, these lights were integrated under a single glass cover.

From the side, the competition cars were smooth with no sculpting. On the production cars, however, there was significant design work, all of which served to make the cars look more muscular. Instead of a plain side, Mercedes-Benz added "eyebrows" over the wheel arches, which both flattened

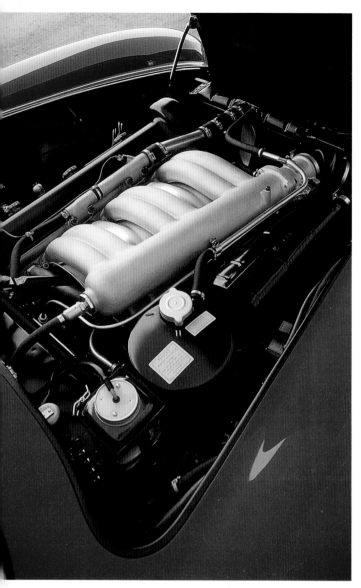

In the production 300SL, the engineers opted for fuel injection, giving the car a 20-horsepower boost over the racing versions. Unfortunately, the induction tubes hide the rest of the engine.

For a car that was derived from a racer, the 300SL coupe was remarkably civilized. Leather upholstery complemented the leather trim around the dash, and the tasteful two-tone instrument panel has a full complement of white-on-black gauges. With its high sills, entering and exiting a Gullwing was difficult. To ease the process, the steering wheel was hinged to tilt. In the race cars, the wheel was removable.

the tops of the arches and gave the illusion of movement while the cars were standing still. To help remove the engine heat, large rectangular vents were installed, with three-by-four square grilles in the fenders. Chrome identification labels told passersby what they were looking at. Both the front wheel "eyebrows" and the large cooling vents had been used on

the 300SLR coupe for Uhlenhaut, except that in the 300SLR, the exhaust also exited out the right vent.

Wheels were bolt-on steel discs, the same as on the 300 sedan. Rudge knock-off center-lock, racer-type wheels were optional. The 300 sedan also was the source for the recirculating ball steering and the four-speed manual transmission.

The Mercedes-Benz 300SL "Gullwing" coupe production car was derived from the racer. Therefore, creature comforts were not the priority of the designers. If passengers wanted to go anywhere for any length of time they needed the optional, fitted leather luggage that stowed behind the seats.

LEFT
Because of the triangulated space frame that ran high through the car's bodyside, conventional doors would not work. The solution was doors that opened with hinges near the roof centerline, giving them the appearance of a bird's wings when they were opened.

BELOW
The production 300SL was based on a car that was originally intended to be raced in 1953. Unlike the cars that did make it to the starting line, the 1953 prototype had a fuel-injected engine, cooling vents in the front and rear fenders, and a simple grille dominated by the three-pointed star.

Bodies on the production cars were primarily steel, with aluminum "moving members" (hood, doors, and trunk lid). After 1956, 29 special, lightweight, all-aluminum production cars were built, which were 176 pounds lighter than the steel cars.

While the competition car had a removable steering wheel to aid in entry and exit, this would not work in a production model. Instead, the two-spoke, 16.5-inch diameter wheel was hinged to allow it to swing down and ease entry and exit.

Matching the ivory of the steering wheel was a similar gearshift knob. This was attached to a vertical, remote lever, unlike the long, angled levers in the prototype and early production cars.

Instruments were clustered in front of the driver, with a large tachometer and speedometer dominating the dash. Below these were the accessory gauges (for fuel, oil pressure and temperature, and water temperature). Unmarked switches and controls were arrayed along the bottom of the dash in a chrome strip, and a clock was placed in the center of the dash. All

continued on page 44

PREVIOUS PAGE
Entering and exiting a 300SL was a challenge, from the driver s or passenger s side. The high sill necessitated a long first step, but fortunately also provided a spot to sit on as you slide in.

continued from page 41

300SLs were left-hand drive, and on extra horn button was located infront of the passenger.

The race cars had had plaid, cloth upholstery, and this was the standard upholstery for the production car as well. Leather upholstery was optional. Few cars were sold in the United States with the plaid, and few restored cars have plaid upholstery. With a list price of $6,820 in 1955, this was one of the most expensive cars of its time. A comparable Jaguar XK140 cost $4,090 at most, and the Aston Martin DB2-4 was $6,295. The Lincoln Continental Mark II was an outrageous (for the time) $10,000. The value of a well-restored 300SL coupe can be many times that price today. Cloth seats simply won't do.

The area behind the two passenger seats was used for storage, since trunk space was taken up almost entirely by the spare tire and fuel tank. Mercedes offered two fitted leather luggage pieces for the well-equipped owner.

Some reviewers complained about the location of the rearview mirror, which was mounted on the dash. While it had a dimming feature to reduce the effect of high beams from cars behind, the view was

The 300SL began the long tradition of a simple grille graced by a three-pointed star.

Taillights on the original road-going 300SL were simple and elegant, unlike the complicated lenses of the third-, fourth-, and fifth-generation cars.

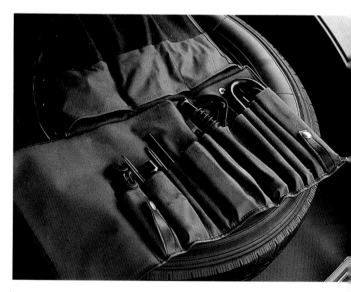

For the home mechanic, or in case of emergencies, each production 300SL carried a standard tool kit that contained the essentials for helping the driver/owner out of most minor jams.

Mercedes-Benz recognized many of the problems inherent in the 300SL coupe (top) and corrected them in the Roadster (below). Among the changes were more compliant rear suspension and conventional doors. In comparing the two cars, it is obvious that the Roadster's doors are significantly deeper, thanks to a modified space frame.

In most restoration shops, several jobs are in progress at the same time. Here, a 300SL frame sits beside a coupe body and a completed Roadster. The best restorations begin by removing the body, drivetrain, and suspension and starting from the base frame. In the case of the 300SL, any weak frame rails are replaced and rewelded, any rust is removed, and the space frame is painted to inhibit any future rust damage. Similar care is used in restoring the upholstery and body. The car is then meticulously reassembled.

poor. One reviewer suggested mounting the mirror from the roof, but since nothing followed a 300SL for long, it wasn't really important. Forward visibility was excellent over the low hood with its two bulges one for engine clearance, one for effect.

There were vertical handles at both ends of the dash and handles on the doors to help pull them down once you were inside the car.

With the same wheelbase, slightly narrower track, and heavier tube chassis to aid production and for the addition of mounting locations, the 300SL was about as close to the race-bred 300SL as you could get. But it was far more civilized.

Ludvigsen again: "To the men of the *Rennabteilung*, the luxuriously trimmed production 300SL was a 'boudoir on wheels' compared to the racer that had spawned it. With its unsurpassed speed, its acceleration still strong high up in the three-figure region, and its exotic looks and technical features, the 300SL hit the motoring world with the impact of a sledgehammer."

Road & Track said:

Few cars have been so long anticipated or so long awaited as the first genuine sports car from Mercedes in over 20 years. Oftentimes a

Taillights on the 300SL Roadster wrapped around the fenders to serve as side-marker lights, whereas on the Coupe they were much smaller. The Roadster's top fit underneath a metal panel behind the seats when it was lowered. There was also more usable trunk space in the Roadster, thanks to a reshaped fuel tank and relocation of the spare tire beneath the trunk floor. Mercedes still offered fitted leather luggage as an option on both cars.

From this angle, the 300SL Roadster's tapering rear end is obvious. This view also clarifies the length of the trunk section. Length does not equal carrying capacity, unfortunately. Even though the Roadster carried more than the Coupe, only two pieces of specially fitted luggage would go in the trunk; two additional pieces would go behind the front seats.

190SL

Among SL and Mercedes-Benz cogniscenti, the 190SL is whispered about as if it were the ugly stepchild, a low-performance car in a long line of high-performance cars.

But this isn't totally fair. True, the 190SL was the only four-cylinder SL (before the 1998 SLK), it had the smallest engine of the line, and it appeared beside the roaring 300SL, which was arguably the best sports car ever, certainly the best sports car of its time. The 300SL production car evolved from the racing sports car of the early 1950s under the direction of Rudolf Uhlenhaut; the 190SL, on the other hand, was developed from a production sedan under the direction of Fritz Nallinger. But while the 300SL grew out of the 300S, the 190SL's parentage was more humble, namely the 180 sedan, the most compact and cheapest of the Mercedes sedans.

But the 190SL, though styled to look like its more storied sibling, was never designed to replace or compete with the race-bred 300SL. It was equipped with a four-cylinder 1,897cc engine to make it a more affordable *alternative* to the 300SL. In this capacity, it more than achieved its goals, bringing a lot of money into DBAG.

When Mercedes-Benz built the 300SL, it didn't exactly build a car for the masses. The 300SL was expensive and out of the reach of most car buyers. The 300SL Roadster, for example, was priced at $10,928 in 1958, compared to $5,232 for the 190SL. For comparison, a 1958 Austin-Healey 100-Six cost $3,389, a Jaguar XK150S $5,120, and a Chevrolet Corvette $3,621. There was a solution to this problem, however: build a less expensive version of the 300SL. The car that resulted from this fairly simple idea was the 190SL. True, the 190SL didn't have the panache of gullwing doors, it had a simple four-cylinder engine rather than the 300SL's exotic, inclined, inline six, and it was relatively inexpensive, which immediately cut back on its exclusivity. But because it was affordable, Mercedes-Benz sold over 25,000 examples of the 190SL. As Frank Barrett wrote in *Illustrated Mercedes-Benz Buyer's Guide*, "Its top didn't leak, it was comfortable, quiet, dependable, warm in the winter, and everything worked all of the time." These were accolades the 300SL never received. "But it was a slug," he added recently.

An early prototype of the 190SL debuted at the New York Auto Show with the 300SL. The car that reached production in January 1955, however, was quite different. New York Mercedes-Benz distributor Max Hoffman was the angel behind the development of the 190SL and probably sold most of the 25,881 cars that were built. His was also the guiding force behind the development of the 300SL, so it's fitting that the production version of Mercedes' greatest racing car and a prototype for smaller, less expensive versions were together on the show stand.

From a styling standpoint, the 300SL and the 190SL were obviously related. There were similar

---

True, the 190SL wasn't a 300SL, but it had a beauty of its own. The 190SL, competed on equal terms with the numerous British sports cars of the time. Its only difficulty was living in the shadow of the 300SL.

"eyebrows" over the wheel arches and the classic three-pointed star floating in the center of an open grille, seemingly suspended by a horizontal chrome strip.

But present Mercedes-Benz design director Bruno Sacco feels the 190SL was "weakly styled" when compared alongside the 300SL. The 190SL resembled the larger 300SL, but it had regular doors, as in the 300SL Roadster. The prototype 190SL had an air scoop in the hood and clean rear fenders. By the time the car reached production, the air scoop had been replaced by a slight bulge in the hood (matching the twin bulges in the 300SL's hood) and flashings over the front and rear wheel arches. Unlike the original 300SL, though, it had optional leather-faced bucket seats (early production versions had cloth-upholstered seats, much like on the 300SL). Later models used a standard seat upholstered in M-B-Tex vinyl or leather. Like the larger Roadster, the 190SL also had a custom-fitted hardtop that became available in September 1959.

L.J.K. Setright, in his book *Mercedes-Benz SL & SLC*, called the 190SL a "vapidly pretentious sibling" to the 300SL. "The poor thing was scarcely powerful enough or fast enough to get itself into any kind of trouble anyway, and might comfortably be dismissed from any consideration of what a sports car ought to be able to do."

Road & Track, on the other hand, diplomatically said that performance was "a function of intelligent use of the gearbox. Driven vigorously through the gears, it gets out and moves. Driven properly through the gears, it is difficult to tell that this is a four."

Though use of existing 180 sedan parts was the goal, use of the sadly underpowered sedan engine (52 horsepower) simply would not do. Instead, a new four-cylinder engine, with the same bore as the six in the 300SL was introduced for the 190SL. Because the 190SLs engine compartment was more than two inches taller than the 300SL, this engine was mounted vertically rather than canted to the side.

The 190SL's 1,897cc four was rated at 120 SAE horsepower at 5,700rpm. While it had a modest top speed of about 105 miles per hour and could reach 60 miles per hour from rest in 13.5 seconds, it wasn't a great performer. The U.S. version of the engine was slightly more powerful at 125 horsepower at 6,000rpm. The 190SL was the first Mercedes with an overhead-cam four-cylinder engine, in this case driven by duplex roller chains with tensioners. Two Solex carburetors fed by an air "ram" that filtered incoming air took care of fuel mixing chores. Compression ratio was 8.5:1. Daimler-Benz used an

From head on, the casual observer might have difficulty determining if the approaching car is a 190SL or 300SL. The differences are in the hood bulges (the 190SL has a single, central bulge the 300SL has two) and in overall size.

air ram in many engines and was researching adjustable-length air rams for the 300SLR when it terminated its official racing program in 1955. (The object of changing ram length was to extend peak torque over a wider range of engine revolutions.)

The engine was mated to a four-speed manual transmission with a floor-mounted shifter, unlike the column-mounted shifter in the sedan, although the prototype had the shifter mounted on the column. Brakes were outboard drums, again from the 180, but they were wider than the sedan's and wore cooling fins.

What held any performance ideas in check was a rather heavy curb weight of 2,557 pounds, plus

The four-cylinder 190SL was offered by Mercedes as a more affordable alternative to the 300SL. While it had some similar styling cues (the "eyebrows" over the wheel openings, for example), its smaller, considerably less powerful engine did not help the car gain respect.

Powering the 190SL was a 1.9-liter, inline, four-cylinder engine that was rated at 105 horsepower. Compared to a Triumph or MG, it was powerful; compared to the 300SL, though, it seemed anemic.

The 190SL, the little brother in the SL line, debuted at the 1954 New York Motor Show. While it offered many of the same visual cues as the 300SL, its smaller engine proved to be a detriment.

another 44 when the optional hardtop was fitted. That calculates out to over 24 pounds per brake horsepower—hardly figures to inflame the heart of performance enthusiasts.

Despite how portly this all sounds, efforts had been made to keep weight down. The 190SL was Mercedes-Benz's first unibody car, with chassis structure steel body and aluminum doors, engine cover, trunk lid.

To create the 190SL's chassis, engineers shortened the 190 sedan's wheelbase by hacking a 10-inch piece out of the floor pan. The result was a wheelbase exactly the same as that of the 300SL.

The floor of the sedan had a strong center tunnel and two boxed side-members. The center forked into a "Y" at the front and formed the engine area with a front tubular cross-member. Behind the passenger compartment, the sedan's chassis narrowed for the rear suspension and wheels. The center tunnel forked in the rear as well for the rear axle. The rest of the chassis was stiffened.

The 190SL used the sedan's standard suspension, since it had been newly designed from

its predecessor, the prewar 170. Up front were twin unequal-length wishbones with coil springs and telescopic shock absorbers. The rear suspension was an improvement over the original 300SL's, with a new swing axle, with lower trailing arms and coil spring/telescopic shock absorber unit. Many observers said the 190SL's rear suspension was superior to that of the 300SL because of what had been learned over time with the older setup. "Handling and roadholding were of a very high order," according to James Taylor. "Springing was perhaps rather stiff, but the 190SL was the first production Mercedes-Benz to use the redesigned swing-axles with low-mounted single pivot, and it could be thrown about with a good degree of confidence up to the fairly high limits of rear-end adhesion."

And while 300SL (had disc brakes all around), the 190SL used drum brakes at all four corners. But again, the brakes didn't have to work as hard.

Options for the 190SL included a hardtop, which gave the car a decidedly coupe-like look, and fitted luggage. The luggage, which was not unlike the

Studebaker-Packard replaced Max Hoffman's New York-based Mercedes-Benz Distributors, Inc.

special fitted luggage in the 300SL, was by Karl
Baisch or Hepco and consisted of five pieces, three
for the trunk and two for behind the seats. The 190SL
actually had space behind the front seats that was
large enough for an optional seat. As with most sports
cars, though, this seat was designed for only occa-
sional use.

A large speedometer and tachometer dominated
the instrument panel, with three smaller accessory
gauges mounted below. The steering wheel came
straight from the 180, with a chrome ring that worked
the turn signals. The handbrake was also sedan-type,
with a T-shaped handle under the dash. The dash top
was padded, and this padding was extended along the
tops of the doors. A glovebox was fitted on the passenger side along with a dash-mounted grab handle. In
May 1956, a clock was added to the now lockable glovebox door.

Mercedes used a baseball analogy for its New
York Motor Show promotional literature:

The 190SL's instrument panel mimicked the 300SL's, with two
main gauges for tachometer and speedometer and accessory
gauges arranged vertically between them. The dash is typical of
the 1950s with leather trim and painted surfaces. Compare the
large steering wheel and chrome horn ring with a car like the
SL500 of the late 1990s, which has a smaller-diameter, but
thicker steering wheel with the horn integrated into a center
pad that also contains an airbag.

Chief of Design Bruno Sacco has been with Mercedes-Benz since 1958 and became head of design in 1970. The first car whose design he was responsible for was the 1979 S-class and its respective coupe. He admits to being impressed by the 1950 Studebaker Commander, designed by Raymond Loewy.

The stunning, new Mercedes-Benz 190SL production sports car offers three hits—Racing Performance, Luxurious Comfort, and Operational Robustness—and no errors, meaning, no sacrifice of the factory's prime principle: safety. And now the car of your dreams has become a reality, it is here and waiting for you. Designed and built for long-distance driving as well as for short daily city rides, this ultra-smart Roadster offers in spite of its sporty character unusually high riding comfort, dependability, and economy. . . . To lower the weight for racing, both doors can be replaced by light-metal doors with a deep arm cutaway, the windshield can be exchanged against a small plexiglass shield just in front of the driver, and the fold-away top as well as the front and rear bumper can be taken off altogether. But the 190SL also wins by fitting it with a sleek-looking hard-top. It is turned then into a distinguished Club Coupe, offering all the comforts of a luxurious sedan. . . Indeed, three hits and no errors—a Roadster, a Convertible, and a Coupe with no flaws whatsoever.

Unfortunately, the special doors and racing windscreen are extremely rare.

By the time the 190SL made it into production nearly two years after it was shown, there were some changes, some good and some bad. Weight increased slightly, which made the four-cylinder

From the rear, the 190SL exhibits a more delicate tail section than the 300SL. In fact, the back half of the 190SL could have been grafted off a similar-era British sports car.

If you compared the 190SL with almost any other four-cylinder sports car of its time, it offered decent performance to go with its good looks. Where the 190SL suffered was when people compared it with the 300SL, a car that had a distinctly different agenda when it was created. The 190SL was meant to be an economical sports car with a family resemblance to the 300SL, nothing more. The 190SL is something of a model for the new SLK230. Both are powered by four-cylinder engines and are lower-priced than their stablemates.

Even though the 190SL was definitely the "little brother" to the 300SL, every effort was made to give the car the same feel as the bigger car. This is evident in the dash, which has a similar layout to the 300SL Coupe. The instrument panel is dominated by the speedometer and tachometer, with the accessory gauges mounted below. Comparisons with the bigger cars show the same ivory steering wheel with chrome ring and dash-mounted rearview mirror.

engine work harder. Styling changed slightly, with a "power bulge" replacing the air scoop on the hood, "eyebrows" over both front and rear wheel arches, and bumper overriders. Inside, the column-mounted shifter went to the floor, which eliminated the bench seat.

Brian Laban called the 190SL "a clever piece of aspirational marketing and a clever piece of engineering, too. Under the racy skin, the 190SL was a far simpler car than the space-framed, fuel-injected, gullwinged 300, and it used even more production-based components. Once on line, it would be relatively easy and economical to build in respectable volumes, which to a manufacturer means respectable profits."

Richard M. Langworth, in *Mercedes-Benz: The First Hundred Years*, wrote, "Had it been built by anybody else, the 190SL would be regarded today as a classic in its own right," but compared

against the 300SL, with which it shared sales spaces, it paled."

While the 190SL proved to be a commercial success, it was not a sporting success. Its only racing successes were those of John Moore in the 1957 Nassau Speed Weeks, where he beat a Jaguar, an Austin-Healey, and a Triumph TR-2 and an overall win scored in the 1958 Hong Kong Rally.

Brian Laban says the car "just was not quite quick enough or rebellious enough." And while the 190SL wasn't a street racer, it "drifted toward a different image. It was seen as respectable, dripping with quality and even nippy enough for the boulevard cruiser." By 1963, eight years after production began, a new, more interesting SL was on the horizon, and the 190SL was allowed to die a respectable death. Still, its place in Mercedes-Benz history is assured, for if the 190SL hadn't proven to be as popular as it was, there is reason to believe that Mercedes-Benz might not have continued the SL line at all.

THE SL IN MASS PRODUCTION

By 1963 the 190SL and the 300SL Roadster were neither Super nor Light. Compared with the Jaguar E-Type (at about half to one-third the price) the 300SL wasn't competitive either. The 190SL was in a confusing middle ground as well: too heavy to compete with the little guys like MG and Triumph, but too underpowered to compete with the Austin-Healeys and Jaguars.

Mercedes-Benz had two choices. It could either return to the premise of the original 300SL and build a super car out of production components, or it could create a new grand touring sports car that would continue the reputation of the SLs as touring cars rather than super racing cars. Mercedes chose the latter with the W113-platform 230SL, introduced in 1963. The 230SL, in fact, was a compromise between the 190 and 300 and fit nicely in between the two previous models. CAR's reviewer called the 230SL "a comfortable two-seater, not too big and not too costly, fast enough to be exciting but above all beautifully sprung and yet sensational in corners."

Like the Gullwing before it, the 230SL had a distinguishing physical feature. While the car as introduced was a roadster, its removable hardtop had a distinctive dip in its center, thereby earning the car the nickname "Pagoda Roof." In theory, this unique design was said to have been developed to offer tall side windows to create a better-balanced side view while still making for a low roofline from the front

and rear. The roof also proved to be an efficient way to remove rainwater and channel it away from the car. (The Italian designer Zagato used a similar technique with its "double bubble" roofs. Zagato used this form on the Fiat Abarth 750. A recent collaboration between Zagato and Autotech-Japan resulted in the double-bubble-roofed Stelvio, while Mazda also used the styling technique for the 1992 RX-7. The depression in the Zagato roof served dual purposes: a reduction in frontal area and aerodynamic drag while still maintaining good headroom, and stiffening the body structure. Mazda's research showed that the roofline increased airflow over the roof, directing it to the rear spoiler for better adhesion.)

"The development of the 230SL [W113] took place in the time when I began working for Mercedes," remembered Bruno Sacco, "so I was able to participate in it as a young designer. The pagoda roof was developed in response to the need for more headroom when getting in and out of the vehicle. The idea came from Béla Barényi. The design of the W113 took something on the order of eighteen months." The design of the W113 cars has been credited to Paul Bracq.

Barényi had designed a car called the K-55 project, which he began in 1955. This project took its roots from his Terracruiser of the late 1940s, which was an early example of modular construction and interchangeable body parts. The K-55 also used modular construction, a

The 230SL was not a pure sports car as the 300SL had been. With its hardtop option and more creature comforts, it was more of a grand touring car. Top speed was in the neighborhood of 115 miles per hour, which was better than the 190SL but not in the same class as the 300SL. The engine and chassis were based on the 220S sedan.

The 220S coupe carried the engine that would be fitted to the 230SL. Elegance and a lively 120 horsepower six-cylinder engine give this coupe a distinct personality.

trapezoidal body form, symmetrical front and rear sections, interchangeable parts, and new roof styles. Among the roof forms was a flat roof with overhangs that Barenyi claimed had 56 advantages over conventional roofs. Barenyi had patented the pagoda roof idea in 1956 under the title "Vehicle with Removable Hard Top Roof." This patent described a roof with loading capabilities in excess of 2,200 pounds. Use of the pagoda-style roof enabled designers to employ greater glass areas in the side and front windows. While the ultimate expression of the Mercedes K55 may be found in the A-edition, due in 1997, the flat roof also led to the concave roof of the W113.

"[Our] strategic intention was to merge the interesting characteristics from the two sports cars which were to be superseded—the 190SL and the 300SL—in the W113," Sacco continued. "The 300SL was designed to be extremely sporty, whereas the 190SL was strongly influenced by the [sedan] and was therefore more of a touring car. Because the W113 was developed for a customer group 'in between' was the ultimate reason for its success."

With a window area some 38 percent greater than the 190SL, the 230SL appeared at first to be almost on the edge of being ungainly. But the added glass resulted in better visibility improved ingress and egress and head room.

But the hard top wasn't an easy one to remove or install. Reviewers called it beautifully engineered,

and it looked as if it shouldn't come off at all. The top could be released by four levers, one each behind the sun visors and two at the rear. Unlatching the top was a one-person job, but lifting it off required an assistant. Mercedes made the top so airtight, though, that you had to crack the side windows to get any airflow. *Sports Car Graphic* pointed out that the large vents in the dash worked well normally, but with the windows rolled up, airflow was reduced to a trickle. There was a vent above the window of the hardtop, but it didn't aid airflow.

"It is very difficult to classify our 230SL Roadster of 1963," Sacco wrote in *Mercedes-Benz Design*. "It is an attempt to replace the legendary SL Roadster and the weakly styled 190SL with a single successor—a successor with dubious styling yet remarkable success. The pagoda roof is the outstanding styling element, which, unusual though it is, was based on a functional consideration, namely to provide more headroom for passengers when getting in and out. The pagoda roof was not adopted by any other manufacturer. The somewhat coquettish appearance of this car, which was especially appealing to women, caused a shift away from the image of our sports car—far away from the 300SL." The styling was more rectangular than round, which had been the theme of the two earlier cars. This was a departure that would also carry to the Mercedes sedans.

Called "the elegant car with the sporty character" by Mercedes-Benz, the 230SL represented a subtle shift from the testosterone-laden 300SL to a more elegant grand tourer.

Front suspensions were independent with wishbones, coil springs, and telescopic shock absorbers. In the rear was the traditional Mercedes-Benz low single-pivot swing axle and coil springs. Handling was called next to uncanny. "It inspires a feeling of tremendous command and confidence which, even under the hardest cornering, the car always justifies," said the reviewer for *Motor*. "There must be a limit but we never found it."

The 230SL used front disc brakes and rear drums; the later models in the series had disc brakes all around. Contemporary theory suggested that unless a car was very fast or very heavy (or both), it would not need more than front disc brakes. For example, American cars of the era, with the possible exception of the Corvette, hadn't even begun to offer disc brakes as standard equipment at the time, much less four-wheel discs. And since the 230SL was not in

The elevated edges of the "pagoda roof" make it quite easy to get into this sports car. Mercedes designed the tall windows and the high sides of the hardtop roof for ease of entry. These elements also gave the car its distinctive appearance.

With its optional hardtop in place, it is easy to see how the W113 SLs earned the nickname "pagoda roof" cars. The unusual shape of the roofline came about for several reasons, including aerodynamics; the shape helped the air move better over the top of the car.

The 230SL came to the United States with a four-speed manual or a three-speed automatic transmission, here indicated on the left rear of the car. When automatic transmissions became standard for Mercedes-Benz cars, the addition to the nameplate disappeared.

the same class as the Corvette, nor was it particularly heavy, front discs would suffice.

Sports Car Graphics The biggest engineering feature of the cars was their wider track. Bernard Cahier called the 230SL "an outstanding road car because Technical Director (Fritz) Nallinger, Chief Engineer (Rudi) Uhlenhaut and their team of first-class men have the unique and precious background of having produced some of the world's most successful racing cars. They have constantly applied their immense racing experience, plus practical knowledge, to the benefit of a fast, safe, superbly handling series of touring cars, the most recent example being the 230SL."

The 230SL was powered by a 2,306cc inline six, and it evolved over the course of its eight-year life into the 2,496cc-powered 250SL and the final 2,778cc-powered 280SL. All engines were inline overhead cam sixes with Bosch mechanical fuel injection, with power modestly increasing with each new iteration, culminating with the 170-horsepower version in the 280SL. Almost 50,000 W113 series cars were built, making them some of the most popular SLs in history. With its larger engine, the 280SL was the most popular, with a production run of 23,885, followed by the initial 230SL (19,831). The 250SL's production numbers were at 5,196.

The 230SL model run spanned three years from 1963 to 1966. While the model didn't stir sporting

Besides the pagoda roof of the removable hardtop, the W113 SLs were among the first Mercedes-Benz cars with vertical headlight clusters. This headlight arrangement would change in later generations, which required horizontal arrangements to allow lower front ends and more aerodynamic designs. European-spec cars used multiple lights under a single lens; American-spec cars used individual headlights and turn signals.

enthusiasts the way the 300SL did, it did further Mercedes-Benz's touring car prowess by being the first model to have factory-installed air conditioning and an automatic transmission. A four-speed manual gearbox was standard in European versions, while the four-speed automatic was favored in the United States. With the shifter on the center console, it was one of the first examples of a gated, automatic shift pattern. Rather than the straight-line P-R-N-D-L of other automatics, the 230SL's shifter had Park furthest from the dash. Going forward you would notch to the right to get out of Park then go to the left to get into Reverse. Drive was another notch to the left with 4 and 3 straight above. Starting from second required another movement of the lever to the right and up.

Since it was a grand tourer and not an out-and-out racing car, the designers of the 230SL could be generous with the luxury. One reviewer commented on the "glove-soft leather" used on the dash. All wrote about the big, deep wraparound seats with full adjustment, individual air controls for driver and passenger, a lighted glovebox, and good interior lighting. The car had an excellent heating system that was up to the rigors of northern U.S. climates.

But since the car was well-balanced and priced well above the bare-bones level, Mercedes wasn't going to offer bare-bones accommodations, so while it offered good performance and great handling, the driver and passenger weren't going to have to suffer for it.

Even with the supposed "inferior" sporting gearbox, the 230SL could accelerate from 0–60 miles per hour in 13 seconds (11 seconds with the manual box) and had a top speed of over 120 miles per hour. These figures remained fairly consistent through the life of the W113 models, primarily because the larger engines were strangled by ever more stringent emissions controls.

73

The 250SL represented the second generation of "Pagoda Roof" cars, with a new 2.5-liter six-cylinder engine that was equal in power to the 2.3-liter engine it replaced. Greater capacity was achieved by lengthening the stroke to 79 millimeters. The new engine also had seven main bearings and a compression ratio of 9.5:1. While horsepower was the same, torque was increased by almost 10 percent to 174 foot-pounds, and both horsepower and torque curves were now flatter, which meant that the power was useful over a wider range of engine speeds.

The 230SL's inline six was derived from that used in the 220SE sedan. In the sedan, the engine was rated at 120 horsepower, while in the sports car it was rated at 150 horsepower. The increased power came from boring the engine out from 2,195 to 2,306cc, bumping the compression ratio from 8.7:1 to 9.5:1, and fitting a new Bosch fuel injection system with a six-plunger injection pump (versus the two-plunger pump of the sedan) and nozzles mounted directly in the cylinder induction ports.

While the 230SL was the fastest Mercedes-Benz then in current production, it did not have the acceleration capability of the 300SL, which was a development many "sporty" reviewers complained about "Many enthusiasts might regret that the emphasis has shifted from performance to comfort and accommodation," wrote the reviewer for *Motor*.

Sports Car Graphic's reviewer, Bernard Cahier, noted that the square, striking lines of the new model were a complete departure from the rounded shapes of the 190SL and 300SL. "When at the wheel of the 230SL for the first time," Cahier noted, "one is immediately impressed by the sensation of comfort, luxury, and outstanding visibility around you. The convenient instruments are easy to read, the turn sig-

nal, wipers, washers, and lights are all concentrated into one practical stick gadget on the steering column. The engine, although not entirely dead quiet at maximum revs, is very smooth. I tried [the automatic transmission] and liked it very much, even for fast driving." Cahier didn't like the appearance of the handbrake, which he called "crude."

Ian Fraser, writing in the Mercedes-Benz Club of America's *The Star*, called the 230SL a quality car, "but only a very remote relative of the 300SL. The example I drove . . . bristled with the virtues that are inherent in Mercedes-Benz. Well, many of them, at least. Somewhere along the way, Mercedes lost their way in the gear-change department. I was shocked to find that the lever was the antithesis of the 300SL's: imprecise, wobbly, vague. In fact, after the 300SL, Mercedes never again made a car with a good manual gear change; that's why automatics are so popular."

Road & Track evaluated a 230SL with automatic transmission and published the results in November 1965:

> If there's one thing that a Mercedes is, it's comfortable. The seats on this 230SL are among the finest we've seen anywhere. They're not pil-

The engine for the 1971 280SL was a 2,778cc, inline, single overhead cam six rated at 170 horsepower. Even with a curb weight of over 3,100 pounds, the 280SL could accelerate to 60 miles per hour in under 11 seconds and had a top speed of 122 miles per hour.

rally in one, which was a spectacular performance in this demanding event.

Film stars and celebrities flocked to Mercedes-Benz. Among the listed 230SL owners was Peter Ustinov, who not only starred in the movie *Quo Vadis*, but also narrated the comedy album *Grand Prix of Gibralter*, which had "Girling Foss" driving for "Schnorcedes." Moss himself also owned one, and

there is a classic photo of Neubauer waving Stirling and Suzy away from the factory.

Bigger Engines Don't Always Mean More Power

In 1966, the 230SL was replaced by the 250SL, which was the same car with a new 2,496cc, inline six-cylinder engine. This new engine, based on the powerplant used in the 250 sedan series, used seven main bearings—the 230SL engine had used only four—so it was a more robust unit. It also came equipped with a larger fuel tank (21.7 gallons versus 17.2 gallons in the 230SL) and 6x14-inch wheels, a half inch wider than on the 230SL. The 250 engine had been introduced in 1965 in the sedans, but it took another year to make it into the SL.

Also new on the 250SL were four-wheel disc brakes. And the system was a "proper" setup for the times; the handbrake operated a small drum brake, and a valve prevented rear-wheel lockup on slippery roads.

Car and Driver ran a 250SL automatic through its paces and reported on the trip in August 1967. The testers went from 0–60 miles per hour in 9.5 seconds and reached an estimated top speed of 118 miles per hour. An automatic was a good choice for the test because more than half of the second-generation SLs

When compared with the cockpits of later Mercedes-Benz SLs, the 1971 280SL seems very simple. As with most cars of the early 1970s, there is no center console, even though there is a floor-mounted shifter. There is minimal wood trim on the dash, which is the same color as the exterior. The instrument placement, too, is a reflection of past times, harking back to the panels of the 300SL Roadster and 190SL.

were sold with the option, and even more than that in the United States.

> Every driver who has more than a purely utilitarian interest in automobiles should drive a Mercedes-Benz 250SL at least once in his life. The car is an almost perfect yardstick against which to measure any other car. There are cars with better acceleration, cars with better brakes, cars with better roadholding. But there is no car we can think of that has such a remarkably good balance of performance, safety, and comfort, and has them in such an absolutely civilized structure.
>
> Fangio could never win a Mille Miglia in a car like this. But the average inbred aristocrat could drive it from Brescia to Rome and back to Brescia, pass just about everything in sight, post a remarkably high average speed for the trip, and never hear a murmur of complaint from the lady in the passenger seat. As a matter of fact, she'd probably never even lift her nose out of her latest copy of *Paris Match*. And that's what we mean by civilized.

Car and Driver also commented on the car's "extreme stability. Any maneuver is accompanied by a change in the car's attitude . . . which can quickly be observed from the driver's seat."

There was some nosedive when you applied the brakes, that affected stability in turns. In addition,

there was no road shock on rough surfaces or in sudden lane changes, for example. Part of the reason, of course, is that the car was designed to be sprung softly for ride comfort, but it was also the result of good ride tuning by the suspension designers.

The production life of the 250SL was short, only 15 months. It was replaced in November 1967 by the 280SL, with a more powerful version of the W129 engine. In fact, it was so much improved that it gained its own designation: W130.

The 2,778cc inline six developed 170 horsepower at 5,750rpm, up 10 from the 250SL and 20 from the 230SL. The increase in power was attributed to air as a coolant for the oil cooler (as opposed to water cooling), a new block with modified cylinder spacing to improve engine cooling, and a higher (9.5:1) compression ratio. The larger engine also delivered significantly more torque, 193 foot-pounds at 4,500rpm versus 174 foot-pounds at the same revs for the 250.

You could wind the 280SL's engine up to 6,500rpm by manually shifting the automatic in second or third, whereas it shifted automatically from first at 5,800rpm.

Road & Track's August 1968 evaluation of the 280SL, which had risen in price to a shocking $7,536, led off: "Some cars don't change, they just get better."

> The 280SL is a complex car, especially in the engine compartment with the mechanical fuel injection system looking like a graduate project at the Institute of Plumbing Engineers. But it is a well-proven, reliable car, and the quality of its execution is a delight to the connoisseur of fine automotive machinery. It is somewhat paradoxical that this car does not offer the latest engineering developments of Mercedes-Benz—the improved automatic transmission, the anti-dive front suspension or the new semi-trailing rear suspension. . . . In any case it is still a unique and desirable car; for those who have less than $10,000 to spend and value finesse, pure quality, and drivability more than jazzy looks, it is alone in the field.

According to Frank Barrett, in the *Illustrated Mercedes-Benz Buyer's Guide*, "Sixty percent of 230SLs had manual transmissions, and air conditioning was then unavailable. A 280SL was far more likely to have an automatic transmission and Frigiking air conditioning."

All W113 cars were unibody construction, with steel bodies and aluminum doors, hoods, and trunk lids.

The seats were claimed to be "orthopedically designed," with adjustable backrest controls, which were easy to reach, including those for the heating/air conditioning system. In its ads for the car, Mercedes-Benz said it offered "all the pleasures of sports car driving—and none of the privations. It does not resemble a rocket-ship or a fugitive from a racetrack. It is sporty, but deliberately unflashy. It is a civilized sports car. For grown-ups. Inside, the car is proportioned for everyday adults, not acrobats. The cockpit is lavishly finished in rugged MB Tex or (optional) rich leather—including, of course, the interior of the glovebox."

The safety efforts of Béla Barényi continued. Modifications to the 280SL included a revised steering hub and an energy-absorbing steering column and three-point seatbelts.

Many reviewers of the era were impressed by the silence of the 280SL's engine, even at speeds approaching 100 miles per hour. Jerry Sloninger, writing in *Wheels*, compared the 250SL engine with that of the 280SL by noting that the smaller engine "seemed almost frantic by 280SL standards." Sloninger also drove the 280SL at speeds in excess of 115 miles per hour for long stretches with no pain to the car or his ears.

Handling was very good for a road car, but less than one would want for a race track. The rear suspension was the swing axle that Mercedes-Benz had used for years, and though this same arrangement induced oversteer in Volkswagen Beetles, the heavier front end of the Mercedes plus the low pivot points of the axle offered better control. This was not a car that you could drive hard into a turn, then change your mind and back off the throttle mid-corner; such behavior would cause the rear end to come around. It was better to keep your foot in it and drive through the corner.

The recommended power steering was considered to be the best of its era, which contributed to near-neutral handling with a quick response to any steering input.

In its initial test of the 280SL in August 1968, *Road & Track* said the ride over all sorts of roads was fantastic, with a rigid and rattle-free body. "The supple suspension just works away down there without disturbing the superb poise of the SL."

A survey of 230/250/280SL owners by *Road & Track* proved interesting. A good majority of owners (56 percent) said they drove their cars hard; 35 percent said they drove moderately; and only 8 percent said they drove very hard. More than 70 percent owned other cars. Owners said they bought the cars because of Mercedes-Benz reputation for quality, careful assembly, and good materials. Only 9 percent said that safety played a part in their decisions. The main factors in the buying decision were handling (33 percent) and styling (32 percent), followed by comfort (21 percent) and previous ownership (19 percent).

In June 1969, *Road & Track* comparison-tested the 280SL with a Corvette, Jaguar XKE, and Porsche 911T and found the Mercedes to be the slowest in acceleration, top speed, and fuel economy. *R&T* said the image was "Square. Well built. High class engineering. Nothing frivolous. Strictly functional. Even dull." As solid and well-behaved as the 280SL was, though, it was time for Mercedes-Benz to tread the path of its competition and install a V-8 engine in its beloved sports car. The next-generation cars would be powered by a variety of V-8 engines before it was time for them to pass the baton.

As with the 300SL Roadster and the 190SL, the soft top of the 280SL would stow behind the seats when lowered. The new car tended more toward luxury than pure sport. The steering wheel was flattened slightly at the bottom to make entry and exit easier. Secondary instruments were in a vertical cluster between the speedometer and tachometer, while a touch of wood trim adds to the luxury trappings.

THIRD-GENERATION CARS:
V-8 POPULARITY

The 300SL and its brothers were spectacular cars. The Gullwing design, outstanding racing record, and elegant Roadster successor not only returned Mercedes-Benz to a successful competition mold, they also gave the company the "halo effect" it needed to springboard itself back into a position as a major manufacturer.

The second-generation 230-280SL cars a slightly ungainly side profile that offered ease of entry and exit. And these cars had a unique styling feature as well, the "pagoda roof" of the detachable hardtop. What would Mercedes offer to follow up?

Mercedes-Benz replaced the W113 "Pagoda Roof" cars after an eight-year run—long by some standards but about average for Mercedes. Six years and millions of dollars in development went into creating the next generation. The new SLs was designated R107, and the first of that line was the 350SL, introduced in June 1971. The series would run to 1989 and would eventually include eight soft-top cars and seven coupes. In fact, the coupes would be the mainstays of the line for the final five years of the R107 line in Europe as Mercedes-Benz prepared for the introduction of a new 300SL.

But we're getting ahead of ourselves.

Mercedes watchers were expecting the ultimate in exciting SLs, and were somewhat disappointed when the R107 cars were announced. What fueled the expectation was the C111 test vehicle—almost a dream car. First shown in April 1969, the C111 was a test bed for Wankel rotary engine development at Mercedes-Benz. Only six C111s were built, all originally fitted with three-rotor Wankel engines. The first developed 280 horsepower, and the rest were rated at 300 horsepower. They gave the 111 a top speed of 165 miles per hour. A later four-rotor Wankel design permitted the C111 to go to 180 miles per hour, heady speeds in those times. Several thousand orders were placed for the car right after it was shown, and one prominent American race driver said he'd sell his soul for a chance to drive the C111 in a race, but it was all to no avail. Though the prototype C111s were production ready with special luggage and even a radio, the car never became a production reality.

No pagoda-roof hardtop distinguished the R107 SLs. In fact, except for the wide variety of engines and phenomenal sales success, the third-generation SL cars can be said to have had no distinguishing characteristics. *Sports Car World* correctly noted that the 1974 generation of Mercedes SL cars confirmed the direction the line had been moving. "Today they are essentially two-seater sedans, which is a hell of a long way from being two-seater sports cars," the magazine said. But isn't that what the SL buyer was looking for?

Road & Track offered the opinion that if one looked at the 350SL, one would say. "Ah, the new Mercedes-Benz," which is what the designers were

---

The 350SL was equally at home in a golf course parking lot or on a back road. With traditional Mercedes-Benz ruggedness to match its luxury, you might find a R107 SL anywhere. The R107s were the only ones to use lower bodyside moldings. While this molding did reduce minor body damage and paint chips from stones, it was abandoned in the next-generation cars. By that time, of course, better paints had been developed that were more chip resistant.

After months of laboratory tests, the 350SL was ready for testing in everyday traffic conditions, camouflaged to hide its true identity. Ready at last for the public, it was introduced in late 1971 and was immediately judged one of the "Ten Best Cars in the World" by *Road & Track* magazine.

seeking. There's a lot to be said for making a new design look as much as possible like the one it's replacing.

"With the SL and SLC of 1971, we introduced the predecessors of our last generation of vehicles," wrote Bruno Sacco in *Mercedes-Benz Design*. "The horizontal affinity of this whole range of products is characterized primarily by the horizontal front light units, which at the same time form an optical unit with the SL face and the radiator grille. The SL and SLC are well-proportioned vehicles, the SLC being without a doubt the more harmonious of the two. Without its coupe roof the SL is still an acceptable vehicle today [1996], even if it is obviously somewhat long in the tooth."

During development at Mercedes, the R107 was referred to as *der Panzerwagen*, or tank because of its curb weight of 3,410 pounds, nearly 300 pounds heavier than the car it replaced. Other dimensions were close to those of the W113 cars, emphasizing the evolutionary changes preferred by Mercedes-Benz engineers.

Bruno Sacco said recently that the development of the R107 and W116 S-class sedans was strongly influenced by the growing need for active and passive safety measures during the era. "The S-class," he remembered, "brought the development, for example, of firmer bodywork structures, [tail]light lenses

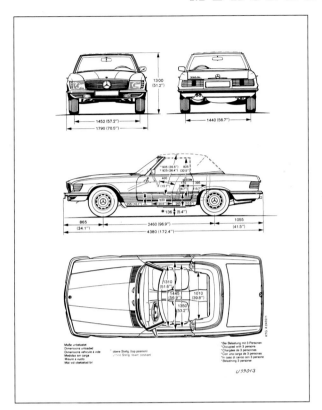

Line drawings of the 350SL indicate basic dimensions and the seating capacity. An optional third seat offered for the 350SL, permitted a rear passenger to sit sideways, but it is very rare.

window line. On soft-top versions, the canvas retained a more normal shape with a three-window back.

When the final design appeared, the car was slightly larger all around than the previous generation, beginning with a wheelbase that was 2.5 inches longer. These extra inches created space behind the front seats for two jump seats that were suitable for children or luggage. The cars were wider as well, but weren't taller. In fact, the third-generation cars were about 0.25 inch lower. Despite bigger exterior dimensions, the 107SLs seem less roomy inside.

Gone were the vertical headlight stacks that surrounded the grille, replaced by horizontal units that added to the impression of width. These units contained the turn indicator lights as well and wrapped around the sides to serve as side-markers. Initially, the United States cars had to do with twin round headlights. For the first time the taillights had the ribbing that emphasized width and kept the lenses clean by

less prone to soiling, and the prevention of build up on the side and rear [windows]. These features also characterize the SL."

Mercedes-Benz saw its marketing emphasis in the early 1970s shifting away from sport and toward luxury and safety. American safety and emissions regulations aided in this decision somewhat, as there was a trend during the life of the cars away from convertibles and toward hardtop models.

"New and pending U.S. Federal regulations meant that all types of cars were about to become stronger, safer, and less polluting even if, ironically, that meant that first they had to go through a phase of becoming bigger, heavier, and less efficient," wrote Brian Laban.

Leading the development team for the new project were Rudi Uhlenhaut (for the final time), with Chief Engineer Dr. Ing. Hans Scherenberg. Design of the new car began in 1967, and the ultimate shape emerged a year later. There was a subtle wedge shape to the profile. The hardtop roof retained a subtle pagoda shape but had its own upswept rear side

The engine for the 350SL was a 3,499cc V-8 that delivered 200 horsepower at 5,800rpm when it was introduced in 1971. Later versions of would carry V-8 engines as large as 5.6 liters. The engine compression ratio would drop and horsepower would decline as Mercedes-Benz coped with American emission regulations. Even with the 3.5-liter engine, this car was capable of a top speed of over 120 miles per hour.

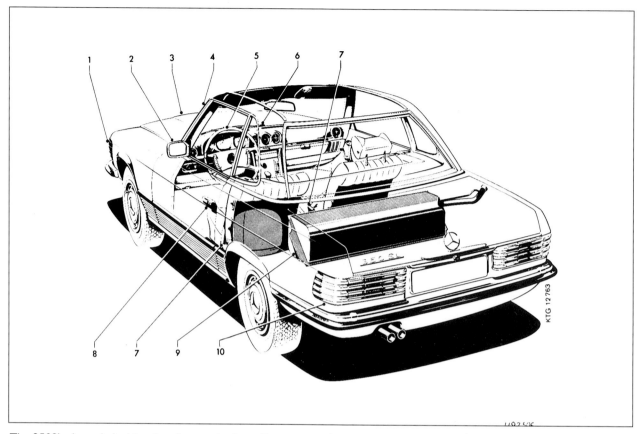

KTG 12763

The 350SL abounded with safety features, such as: 1) wraparound turn signal indicators; 2) breakaway outside mirror; 3) rear-pivoting hood; 4) extra-strong A-pillars; 5) slip-proof steering wheel with power steering standard; 6) wide-sweep wipers; 7) seat-anchored seatbelts; 8) pull-type safety handles; 9) fuel tank recessed deep within the body; 10) wraparound taillights with self-cleaning features.

The elegant instrument panel of the 350SL. The dash is padded leather, and the steering wheel is padded, even if it doesn't contain an airbag. Instruments include speedometer, tachometer, fuel level, water temperature, and oil pressure gauges. A three-speed automatic transmission was standard.

funneling air through the "inside" of the lens to blow away any accumulated dirt. Since this area was deeply recessed, it was also less prone to soiling by airborne dirt or splashed-up mud.

While flush chrome bumpers were adequate for the 350SL in 1971, by 1974 the bumpers had been extended front and rear, much like the extensions that ruined the appearance of the MGB. Mercedes moved the R107's fuel tank forward, from under the trunk floor to a spot above the rear axle and between the rear wheels.

U.S. safety regulations decreed that 1974 cars must be able to withstand collisions of 5 miles per hour in the front and 2.5 miles per hour in the rear without damage to the

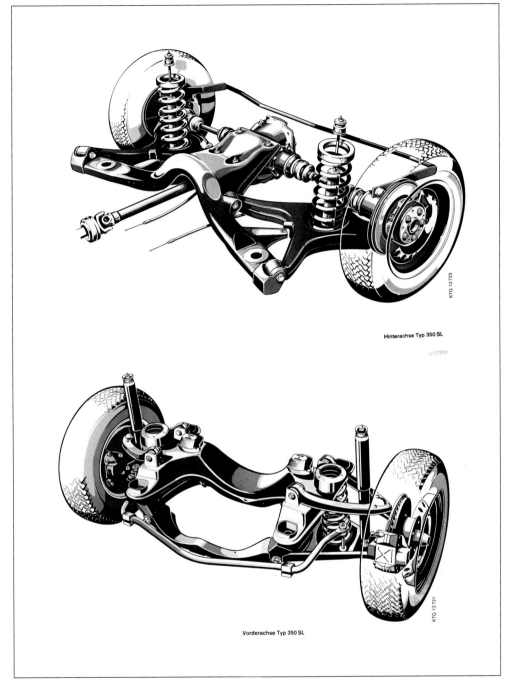

Hinterachse Typ 350 SL

KTG 12723

Vorderachse Typ 350 SL

KTG 12721

The 350SL suspension used upper and lower A-arms in front with tubular shock absorbers, coil springs, and an anti-sway bar. In the rear was a diagonal pivot axle and semi-trailing arms with coil springs, tube shocks, and an anti-sway bar.

lights, fuel tank, or other safety-related systems. Most manufacturers answered the regulations with more metal, and the trend was toward "battering ram bumpers," as *Road & Track* described them. Bigger bumpers mean bigger supports and brackets, ad infinitum. And while Mercedes-

Benz had been practicing the use of deformable structures as a way of protecting the occupants of its vehicles for years, it still had to comply with the federal regulations.

The front and rear impact protection did not detract from the beauty of the car as much as it did

continued on page 90

87

After the stacked headlights of the W113 SLs, Mercedes designers went to horizontal pairs of headlights for the R107 cars. In Europe, the headlights were large rectangular units incorporating both standard and high beams. These lights would not be approved in the United States until well after this 1971 car was imported. Turn signal lights "went around the corner" to also act as side-marker lights.

Unlike the original 300SL or even the 190SL, the 1973 450SL was a far more angular car. Its clean lines, however, characterize it as pure Mercedes-Benz and clearly from the studios of Bruno Sacco. The third-generation R107 cars had a lower front fascia thanks to the horizontally stacked lights.

Inside the 450SL was typical Mercedes-Benz luxury, with leather-upholstered seats, tasteful wood trim, and the best in accessories. Note the classic white-on-black analog instruments—a hallmark of Mercedes-Benz design for decades.

continued from page 87

with some other cars that were hastily modified to conform. Even the windshield pillar of the Mercedes was designed through computer analysis to be strong enough to provide support in the event of a rollover, but still slim enough for styling. The A-pillars also had a profile designed to improve aerodynamics as well as keep water and dirt from the side windows. And in clairvoyant anticipation of as yet unwritten 1998 regulations, the doors were designed to resist side impacts, but without internal reinforcement.

The retarded spark advance, lean fuel mixtures, and low compression ratio required to reduce nitrogen oxides in the exhaust sucked away all the power. Therefore, Mercedes kept the unmodified 3.5-liter engine for European use and created a 4.5-liter version for American SLs by using the same bore and adding

almost 20 millimeters to the stroke (65.8 millimeters to 84.7 millimeters). With the added liter of displacement and a lower compression ratio created by enlarged combustion chambers in the head, the 4.5-liter engine could operate on unleaded fuel and meet 1974 emission regulations three years early. Therefore, the power was the same for the two engines, but the 4.5-liter did it at a lower engine speed.

Transmission choices were different between Europe and the United States as well. In Europe, buyers could choose between a four-speed manual or four-speed automatic. In the United States, only the three-speed automatic was available initially. According to Allan Girdler, writing in *Road & Track*, "Because of the variation in engine speeds and loads, the engine would need a second set of spark plugs and fuel calibrations and a second set of certification tests" for two transmission choices. And since research showed that only 30 percent of 280SL buyers chose the manual, Mercedes rode with the majority and only offered the automatic.

Performance was exciting even if it wasn't outstanding. The factory claimed a top speed in excess of 130 miles per hour and a 0–60 miles per hour time of less than 8.5 seconds.

These new cars weren't new versions of the vaunted 300SL. In fact, most people didn't even think they deserved the name "sports car." *Sports Car World* wrote, "The latest SL range only confirms the direction in which the Benz two-seaters have been moving. Today they are essentially two-seater sedans, which is a hell of a long way from being two-seater sports cars." They added, "Mercedes has obviously discovered that a large number of people with $20,000 to spend on a car don't want an exotic appearance. They probably want a relatively mild look to satisfy their conscience that their 20 grand sporty car is practical and not an 'irresponsible' Dino."

While the engine and body shape were an evolution from the previous design, the suspension was greatly improved over the W107 cars. The front suspension was by upper and lower A-arms, coil springs, and tubular shocks. In the rear, Mercedes replaced the old low-pivot swing axle with semi-trailing arms, coil springs, and tube shocks. Sway bars were installed at both ends to increase roll resistance and smooth out the ride.

The trailing arm rear suspension was similar to that used on other Mercedes-Benz coupes and sedans.

Brakes were power-assisted four-wheel discs, with the front discs being ventilated. Anti-lock brakes

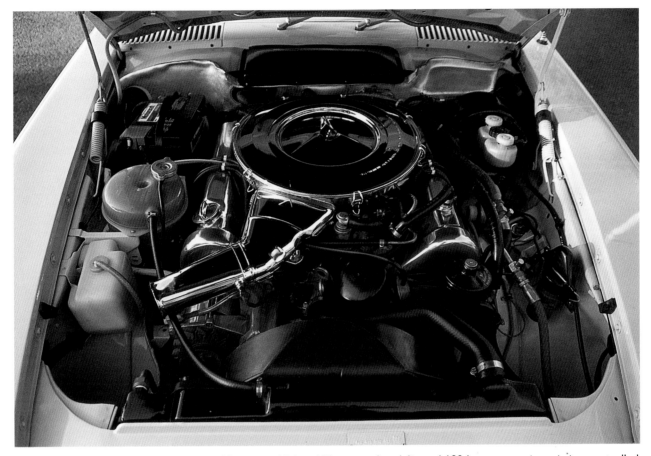

At the heart of the second-generation 450SL was a 4.5-liter V-8 engine that delivered 180 horsepower in emission-controlled U.S. trim. The 450SL sold from 1973 to 1980, smack in the middle of fuel economy concerns and worry over emissions. It would be several years before manufacturers overcame the challenges presented by these twin demons.

(ABS) were not available for the first models in 1971, but became available in the U. S. in 1989.

Inside, driver and passenger rode in the customary soft, wraparound Mercedes-Benz seats. Both seats offered adequate adjustment so that even the tallest drivers could be comfortable. In addition, the driver's seat was adjustable for height. The seats were separated by a high and wide console that contained many of the controls, giving each occupant half of the cockpit to control. Lap and shoulder belts were provided with inertia reels. Most reviewers complained about the steering wheel, which several called "enormous."

Despite its detractors, who wept for the loss of the SL's sportiness, this third generation proved to be as popular commercially as the previous one, with total sales of over 155,312 for the convertible versions and almost 55,000 for the coupes. Still, it was undeniable that something had been lost. As if to counter any criticism, Mercedes-Benz introduced the 350SL

at the Hockenheim race circuit. Rudi Uhlenhaut was there to offer demonstration rides.

Ian Fraser, writing in *The Star*, noted:

> The extraordinary thing about the new-generation SL was that it was to soldier on for almost two decades, acquiring and discarding engines and minor improvements as the years progressed. What started as a 350SL ended as a 560SL, having reverted along the way to the old

continued on page 94

Next pages
The 450SL exhibits a subtle wedge shape in pure profile, again for aerodynamic purposes. The car had a list price in the United States of $11,688 and a top speed of 113 miles per hour. This was sufficient for the 450SL, as it was sold in the era of the nationwide 55-mile-per-hour speed limit.

Mercedes-Benz offered the 4.5-liter engine of the 450SL almost from the start in the United States. Emission control strangulation meant the American 450SL developed about the same horsepower as the European 350SL, albeit at a lower rpm. Torque was increased to 279 foot-pounds. The 450SL was offered only with a three-speed automatic transmission.

continued on page 91

2.8-liter twin-cam six as a kind of economy model to fill a market need for lower fuel consumption in the wake of the 1974 fuel crisis.

Even MBAG engineers were alarmed by its longevity but also surprised by the public's loyalty to an old, world-weary design. Logic suggested that there should have been one, or maybe two, completely new SLs between 1971 and the car's farewell in 1989.

Wheels wrote, "The Mercedes 350SL is one of the most baffling cars to write about because there is nothing with which to compare it. On paper, the specification seems to be all wrong and you wonder who would buy it but, just as the bumblebee defies the laws of aerodynamics and continues to fly despite calculations that say it can't, the 350SL sells in a very successful manner."

Europeans had a chance to drive the 4.5-liter version of the 350SL beginning in 1973, when the 350SL 4.5 officially became the 450SL. Horsepower was down to 190 in the United States, though, as emissions regulations continued to sap power. Initially, the only gearbox available in the United States was the three-speed automatic, but a four-speed automatic became available with the introduction of the 380SL in 1980.

In 1976, the 280SL came back to life in an R107 body in Europe. The 2,746cc inline six was rated at 177 horsepower initially. In 1985, with fuel economy and emissions regulations becoming less stringent

Instrumentation in the 1974 450SL consists of a large speedometer in front of the driver, smaller tachometer off to the right, and accessory gauges to the left. By 1974, it was doubtful that the full range of the 160-mile-per-hour speedometer could be used, though some testers claimed a top speed of nearly 120 miles per hour.

Mercedes-Benz developed the ribbed taillight lens to keep them clean. Aerodynamics plays a major part in sweeping dirt away from the lens, but the unique design also serves to keep airborne dirt away from the interior parts.

By 1974, when this 450SL was built, extended bumpers that were intended to protect the car in a 5mph collision projected out from the front and rear of the car. The original canvas top on this car exhibits the classic three-window design that offered decent visibility out the rear. But the owner almost never runs the car with the top up, which is why it has been able to survive more than 20 years.

and more controllable, the 280SL gave way to the 300SL. The 2,962cc single overhead cam six developed 188 horsepower in the 300SL, just a bit more than was available in the 280SL.

The 350SL and 450SL were replaced by the 380SL in 1980, with a 3,893cc single overhead cam V-8 rated at 155 horsepower. This car, in turn, was replaced in 1985 by the 420SL, using a 4,196cc V-8 that developed 218 horsepower. Slowly the power was returning.

The 450SL begat the 500SL in 1980 in Europe, with a 4,973cc, 240 horsepower V-8. Five years later, this car was replaced with the largest V-8 in SL history, the 5,547cc, 227-horsepower version in the 560SL. This car was introduced in 1986 with a sticker price of just under $50,000. The 5,547cc engine was rated at 227 horsepower and finally had a four-speed automatic, new front suspension, torque-compensating rear axle with reduced squat and lift, limited slip differential, and ABS—anti-lock brakes. There was also an airbag and built-in anti-theft system. *Road & Track* called the 560SL "a middle-aged hot rod." It was by far the fastest R107.

Coupe (SLC) versions of most of these SLs were introduced along with the convertibles. The 450SLC had an enviable rally record at the hands of Eugen Böhringer, while the 500SLC won the 1980 Bandama Rally in Africa.

The 350SLC, for example, was the first SL to have ABS installed. A Teldix system was the one initially used.

Mercedes-Benz designed the SLCs to be closer to an American hardtop coupe than a hardtop sports car. The side windows rolled down completely and there was no B-pillar. The 14-inch-longer wheelbase allowed for two real seats in the back, rather than the poor excuse for a jump seat that existed in the SL soft tops. With two passengers and a lot of luggage aboard, the SLC had almost ideal 50/50 weight distribution between the front and rear axles. Add two more people and keep the luggage, and the distribution remains about the same, which meant good handling under light and heavy loads. Luggage capacity was also increased 20 percent.

Equipment and accessories for the SLC were in the same class as the SLs and luxury sedans. There was standard air conditioning,

Mercedes-Benz built permanent, hardtop coupe versions of the third-generation SLs. This 450SLC is an excellent example of the genre. Three 450SLCs were entered in the 1978, 30,000-kilometer (18,000 miles) South American Rally. All three cars finished, with 450SL driver Andrew Cowan winning the event.

A Mercedes-Benz SLC-series coupe—the coupe version of the SL sports car—was the five-millionth Mercedes-Benz passenger car produced since 1946. Postwar passenger car production began in 1946 with the 170V.

automatic transmission, power steering and brakes, AM-FM stereo radio with power antenna, leather upholstery, power windows, heated rear window, and fog lights.

Motor compared a later 450SLC with the Jaguar XJ-S, despite the fact that they called the XJ-S a 2+2 and the SLC a true four-seater. "Both cars are luxurious, both cars are beautifully made. The Mercedes is the better finished of the two," they wrote. For performance, the Jaguar got the nod by virtue of its V-12 engine. Overall, the two cars tied in points for performance, economy, handling, brakes, etc. Motor gave the overall edge to the Jaguar because of price.

What the Critics Said

In 1980, Road & Track tested a 450SL, a car that by then had seen 10 years of evolution. By 1980, the

HOT R107s

While the SL had metamorphosed from an all-out racer in its 300SL era to a more sophisticated sports tourer in its third-generation R107 form, Mercedes-Benz still wanted to show that it had not forgotten what competition was all about and that it had not forgotten how to win. Shortly after the introduction of the convertible version of the 350SL, Mercedes-Benz exhibited a coupe version of the car, the 350SLC, at the Paris Motor Show. (Eventually, all the R107 cars would have fixed-head coupe, or C107, versions.) Competition was one of the prime reasons for the creation of a coupe. A soft-top car was not as safe as a hardtop, nor would they compete in the same classes. Mercedes planned to enter these cars in rallies around the world.

One of the first events to witness the SLC was the 1978 running of the 30,000-kilometer South American Rally. Four 450SLCs were entered, powered by 231-horsepower engines and capable of top speeds in excess of 130 miles per hour. Andrew Cowan and Colin Malkin emerged victorious in that event.

In 1979, a 5.0-liter version of the 450SLC–the 450SLC 5.0- appeared in the East African Safari. Hannu Mikkola and Arne Hertz finished second, while Bjorn Waldegaard and Hans Thorzelius placed sixth. The 5.0-liter engine was rated at 290 horsepower and could propel the coupe to more than 135 miles per hour. Mikkola and Hertz took a similar car to the grueling Bandama Rally to close out the season and led a one-two-three-four Mercedes-Benz sweep, encouraging the factory to mount a full rally effort for 1980.

Mikkola and Hertz continued their success by placing second in the Codasur Rally in Argentina in 1980 in a 500SLC. Hans Waaldergaard and Thorzelius won the Bandama Rally later in the year, even though they were competing against smaller and more nimble cars.

At the end of the C107's competitive life, Jochen Maas and Albert Pfuhl entered the Paris-Dakar desert Rally in an essentially unmodified 500SLC. This was an optimistic endeavor, as they had no chance of winning against purpose-built machines like the four-wheel-drive Porsche 911. Maas finished 62nd after an accident that delayed him for almost a day, while Pfuhl finished 44th overall.

There was even the entry of a C107 SL in the SCCA Trans-Am series in 1981 and 1982, entered Neal DeAtley and driven by Loren St. Lawrence. This car reportedly had a 450-horsepower engine, but was not successful competing against the highly modified Camaros and Mustangs of the day.

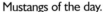

Mercedes-Benz may have withdrawn from official participation on the race track in 1955, but its cars were serious rally contenders for many years, with drivers such as Eugen Böhringer, here shown in an African event.

From this angle, the primary difference between the W107 cars and the previous ones can be seen in the ribbed taillight lenses. Mercedes-Benz points out that this design is "self cleaning."

price was up to $36,130–it had been $10,700 in 1971 and $18,930 in 1976. Partially contributing to the price increase were an automatic climate control system, cruise control, Becker Europa stereo sound system, heated seats, leather upholstery, and metallic paint.

R&T had called the 450SL the "ultimate in a two-seater luxury car" in its first review in January 1977 and continued to call it that in 1980. Performance had suffered as compared to that original model, though. Top speed with the three-speed automatic was only 112 miles per hour, and it took 11.7 seconds to reach 60 miles per hour from a standstill. While reviewers and friends classified the 450SL as heavy, the magazine still

called it "one of the world's great automotive status symbols—and a reliable, well-built, proven one at that."

In the May/June 1996 issue of *The Star*, Ian Fraser wrote that the 500SL "came closer to being a sports car than any others in its immediate family. . . . The big V-8's performance came quite close to the outrageous end of the scale, though, particularly in the context of the year of its European introduction, 1980. A development of the original 3.5-liter V-8 concept, it was in fact a line of engines of which the 380 was at the lower end, of all-alloy construction with a single overhead camshaft in each cylinder head and using Bosch indirect fuel injection. Output was more

Through its 18-year model life, the W107 cars carried several engines of varying displacements. The largest was the 5.6-liter V-8 in the 560SL. This 1988 model is unrestored, but well cared for. With the top down or up it retained the classic profile of the third-generation cars. By 1989, however, the body style had grown long in the tooth, and it was time for a new design.

By the time the R107 cars were nearing the end of their lives, the dash and instrument panel had received some changes. Most obvious is the installation of an airbag in the steering wheel hub. There's also significant wood trim in the center console, which now houses the shifter for a four-speed automatic transmission. Metric markings have been added to the speedometer as well.

Luxury played an ever more important role as the SL evolved. The 560's interior room had not increased over the original 450SL of the third generation, but comfort certainly had. Leather seats were well-padded, there was a driver's side airbag, it had an anti-theft system and heated windshield washer nozzles.

The R107 cars, were among the last designs from stylist Karl Wilfert and technical director Rudolf Uhlenhaut, who retired in 1972. This car has the lower body side cladding typical of the series, designed to protect the body from damage by small stones and tar. Compared with the W113 cars that preceded them, the R107 SL Mercedes-Benzes rode on a wheelbase that was 2.4 inches longer at 96.9 inches, and were 1.3 inches wider at 70.5 inches. Overall length was 172.4 inches in Europe, about 2.5 inches longer than the W113 cars. U.S.-spec cars were ten inches longer, due to extended bumpers.

than enough to propel a European SL to 150 miles per hour and accelerate it—via the four-speed automatic—to 60 miles per hour in 7.5 seconds and to 100 in 16.5 seconds, all as effortlessly as only an understressed V-8 can do it."

But after 18 years of life, it was time for another change. The last R107 car was built on August 4, 1989, at Bremen. It was destined for the Mercedes-Benz Museum in Stuttgart. However, the next-generation cars were already being produced, and these cars would restore some of the sporting character that was lost when the original 300SL ceased production. The new R129 cars would continue with the luxury, though, continuing the dichotomy that has meant SL to automobile lovers throughout the world.

The biggest SL engine before the 6.0-liter V-12 in the 600SL was the 5.6-liter V-8 used in the 560SL. With fuel injection, the 560SL developed 227 horsepower and 279 foot-pounds of torque. It was mated to a four-speed automatic transmission. Top speed was 130 miles per hour, and the car would accelerate from 0–60 miles per hour in 7.5 seconds.

FOURTH-GENERATION CARS: THE SL PUMPS UP

By the late 1980s, the SL name no longer represented the ultimate in sports cars, or even the ultimate in sporting cars. While the 450SL, 380SL, 280SL, and 350SL were fine tourers, they lacked the performance and styling to excite an enthusiast's heart. True, a lot of the blame for the sap in performance can be laid at the feet of the U.S. Environmental Protection Agency, which demanded ever lower emissions. Mercedes-Benz, like many manufacturers, fought reduced power with larger engines, but the results were not always satisfactory.

It was time for a change.

The change Mercedes-Benz had in mind was exciting: restore style and performance to the SL name. The company would do it with a dramatically restyled body and three new engines, in what Mercedes would call the R129. It offered the SL buyers a list of features unavailable in any other car. As one writer put it, the 300SL and 500SL introduced in 1990, "reversed the trend toward bulk, weight, and breathlessness. . . ." in the SL range.

As with many Mercedes-Benz designs, the form chosen for the new SL range was conservative, not avant-garde—evolution versus revolution, if you will. Long design cycles have been a Mercedes-Benz tradition, and in the 35 years from the first 300SL to the introduction of the, there had been only three major designs. As Bruno Alfieri wrote in his summary of the fourth-generation cars, *Mercedes-Benz SL: 300SL,* 300SL-24, 500SL, "Experience has shown that a car design which stands out against others by means of fancy avant-garde form elements is bound to be outdated quicker than those cars which deliberately shun such effects."

Chief Designer Bruno Sacco led the design team responsible for the new SL, and he feels the result was the most attractive SL since the 300SL Roadster of 1957. Among the challenges facing the team was to create a design that would be equally attractive with the top up or down, since the combination of engineering and design had created a near-perfect mechanical top that could be raised or lowered in a matter of seconds.

Among the design elements Alfieri feels are significant in the models are an extended hood reaching down to the front, a short and compact-shaped roof, a compact rear section that still contains flowing lines, even-surfaced sides with an aerodynamic wedge shape, a top construction that forms an aesthetic entity with the body, an organically embedded windshield including the A-pillar, flared wheel arches, and a redesigned radiator grille that retains the SL character in a new, more aerodynamic shape.

In addition, the trapezoidal front light groupings were an integral part of the front fenders and helped define the grille. The grille itself continued the tradition of SL cars, but with modern design elements such as anodized aluminum slats framing the nicely

Present-generation SLs have a muscular exterior look, while still retaining a compact shape. This is a 1996 SL500, with the 5.0-liter V-8 engine. Others in the line are the six-cylinder SL320 and the V-12-powered SL600.

Four versions of the latest-generation SL were available, with the smallest being the six-cylinder 300SL. With Mercedes-Benz's change in nomenclature and an enlarged engine, this became the SL320 in 1995. The least expensive of the modern SLs, it carries a price tag of around $80,000.

integrated three-pointed star. The taillights combined brake signaling, turn signaling, and back-up lights in a pleasing shape that echoed the front lights, while still incorporating Mercedes-Benz's ribbed dirt-free design. The lights wrapped around the sides of the rear fenders to also function as side-marker lights. Below the grille was a new bumper design that incorporated invisible shock-absorbing elements.

The interior of the R129 cars was a combination of functionality and elegance, with an abundance of wood trim, leather, and easy-to-read instruments. Unlike other manufacturers who chose to bathe their instruments in orange light or employ digital gauges, the R129's simple white-on-black analog gauges transmitted the information in a more traditional manner.

The front seats had seat belts mounted to the seats that were a pleasure to use. The inertia-reel belts, combined with belt tensioners and sash guide height adjustments, eliminated any rubbing across the neck, as some belts from other manufacturers are wont to do. And all models had dual airbags to com-

plement the belts, continuing the tradition established by safety guru Béla Barényi. Behind the seats was the worlds fastest automatic roll bar; an integrated wind-deflecting screen eliminated much of the backdrafts encountered in open cars.

While the safety of seatbelts attached to the seats may raise questions, the installation by Mercedes-Benz received high marks from every safety research organization. And well it should. Mercedes-Benz sends teams out to investigate most accidents in Germany involving a Mercedes-Benz vehicle. They have data on over 450,000 accidents and have shared this data with, among others, the U.S. government.

Their results are interesting, especially in the light of how they equip their cars and how the government tells them to equip their cars. For example, the R129 cars have a roll bar that pops into place in 0.3 seconds if a rollover is detected. Yet, research shows that rollovers occur in less than 1 percent of all accidents. Perhaps the roll bar is there to give the passengers a "warm fuzzy" feeling about riding in a soft-top car.

Power for the 500SL came from a 4,973cc V-8 rated at 326 horsepower and 332 foot-pounds of torque. It had double overhead camshafts on each cylinder bank and 48 valves for maximum breathing. The compression ratio was 10.0:1, and Bosch fuel injection managed the fuel delivery. All that power and torque was necessary for maximum performance because the 500SL, as introduced, weighed over two tons, very heavy for a sports car.

When Mercedes-Benz introduced the 500SL in 1989, the new car was obviously a departure from the two generations of SLs that had preceded it. First, it was offered with two engine choices: a 3.0-liter six or a 5.0-liter V-8. Second, it had dual airbags for safety and copious amounts of leather and wood trim. With a four-speed automatic transmission, the 500SL could accelerate to 60 miles per hour in under six seconds, and it was capable of speeds higher than its electronically limited 155 miles per hour.

The U.S. government insists that all manufacturers install beams in their doors to protect the occupants in the event of a side collision. Side airbags, as installed in current Mercedes-Benzes, Volvos, and other cars, are another feature for this type of accident. Yet Mercedes-Benz research shows that side impact accidents occur in only one out of 40,000 accidents.

Mercedes-Benz—as well as precious few other manufacturers—installs the battery in the trunk of the new-generation SL. This is because their research has shown that over 40 percent of all accidents are offset at the left front. These accidents occur when the car is hit by one coming from the other direction. If the battery is in the front in a frontal accident, it could break, or explode, spreading sulfuric acid all over. Its location in the rear is much safer.

Work on the new design began in 1982. Three design directions were pursued: a continuation of the R107 design, more futuristic shapes in the SL mode, and development of the SL concept in a new homogeneous design. The third approach was eventually followed.

Nearly 20 1/5-scale models were built during the preliminary design phase, and several 1:1 wood and clay models were also constructed.

The roof proved to be a particular challenge. Thirty-four different designs were considered before the final one was approved. What resulted was an aerodynamic, watertight soft top that looked good up or retracted into its cell behind the passenger compartment. The top also had to accommodate the automatic sensor-controlled roll-over bar, which would activate if sensors determined a possible rollover situation. This bar, would activate with the top up or down.

In its down position, the roll bar lay flat in front of the soft top storage compartment. While it could be raised manually, it also reacted automatically to any crash situations, much like the airbags. The roll bar extended hydraulically to its full height in just 0.3 second, far quicker than the car itself could roll, offering the passengers excellent protection.

"The rollover bar gives the vehicle maximum safety and enhances its overall rigidity," according to Bruno Sacco. "It is a feature which fits the vehicle concept."

From the side, the R129 cars exhibit a distinct wedge shape, particularly with the top recessed. There was also a link to the past, with modernized versions of the original 300SL-style air scoops behind the front wheel wells.

The 300SL was the smaller-engined of the two initial models. While it retained the glorious name from the past and carried a six-cylinder engine that

One of the best features of the SL500 and its stablemates is the power top. The driver has only to push one button to transform the car from a well-fitted soft-top car to an open-air beauty. The top recesses into a special compartment behind the cockpit, and a metal cover automatically flops back to complete the installation. The whole process takes about 25 seconds.

Behind the front wheels is a strut-type independent suspension with lower wishbones, combined with coil springs and gas-filled shock absorbers. This design offers over seven inches of travel with relatively soft springing. Anti-dive geometry is built into the front suspension. The four-wheel disc brakes are controlled by an anti-lock braking system.

was the equal in power and performance to its legendary namesake, it wasn't the high-performance version of the new SLs.

In European two 300SL versions were offered initially; the European two-valve-per-cylinder 300SL and the four-valve-per-cylinder 300SL-24. The two-valve engine was rated at 190 horsepower, while the four-valve engine developed a healthy 231 horsepower. While the two-valve engine was essentially the same engine as installed in the 300E, the four-valve engine used the same block but with a new head design. The larger 500SL was the most powerful original R129, with a 5.0-liter, 32-valve V-8 rated at 326 horsepower.

In 1995, designations for the entire model line were changed with the SL prefacing the three-digit engine dimension. Thus, the 300SL became the SL300. In 1996, the six-cylinder engine was enlarged to 3.2 liters, creating the SL320 with a 24-valve inline six-cylinder engine rated at a robust 228 horsepower. The 1996 SL500 was rated at 315 horsepower and its ultimate stablemate, the V-12 48-valve SL600, which debuted in 1993, at 389 horsepower.

The V-12 is a very impressive piece. Roller chain-driven, double overhead camshafts actuate the valves, which are mounted at a 50-degree angle. A feature of the engine is the inlet camshaft adjustment, which improves the cylinders' volumetric efficiency depending on engine speed and torque demands. A clutch at the camshaft drive can be activated to affect camshaft timing. The mechanical-electronic fuel injection used on the four-valve engine is also used on the 5.0-liter V-8.

The 190SL was less expensive than the 300SL, but with much of the panache. The SLK230, too, is less expensive than its bigger SL-class brethren, but it retains the familiar styling and performance. *MBNA*

weatherproof coupe. It was meant to be a youthful vehicle that appealed to the emotions—a car which at first sight already suggests sheer driving pleasure.

Involved in this interesting task were approximately 20 designers producing hundreds of sketches. Motivation was never a problem. Some designers were working with clear, straight lines, while other teams designed round, softer forms or modeled their designs on the lines of the 300SL with its distinctive wheel arches.

About 15 designs remained in contention. Those drawings not balancing tradition and innovation were sifted out.

Between October 1991 and January 1992, a 1/5-scale model was produced to transform the designer's ideas into a specific shape. The model makers didn't always stick to every detail of the sketch in front of them. They kept making corrections and minor changes. In automotive design, the transition from the second dimension (sketch on paper) to the third (model) is a clear break. Only then will the truth be discovered, namely whether or not a drawing can stand up to the test of the third dimension.

Five scale models were built and displayed at the Sindelfingen Mercedes Development Centre in September 1992. This was when the final decision was to be made. Only one model would be selected. And with that choice, a lot of design work still remained to be done. In the case of the SLK, for example, the radiator grille and rear window turned out to be too small and had to be reworked.

Then came the moment when the inside and the outside merged. At this point, designers arrived with the final interior design. Once again, sketches and full-scale drawings were followed by clay models and "final mock-ups." Once painted, they gave a fairly realistic impression of the interior.

One morning in March 1993 at the Development Centre, the time had come. The Management Board approved the SLK design.

"Building open-top cars today is not exactly a superhuman feat. But to build an open-top car which is safe and is designed to take the rough with the smooth as a sedan or a coupe, that is something which calls for the innovative strength of the Mercedes-Benz marque—and a sharp intelligence," said Helmut

take a new step toward a design which is characterized more emotionally evocative than merely practical."

It was a long process until the final design touches were applied to the SLK body. Back in August 1991, first sketches for the exterior and interior design were produced. At that time the design brief had not been overly specific: Draw a two-seater sports car with a hardtop that turns the car into a totally

The Mercedes-Benz SLK230 is designed to be a sports car for all seasons and reasons, due in large part to its one-touch retracting hardtop. A 191-horsepower, supercharged engine and sophisticated independent suspension will quickly endear the lightweight SLK230 to sports car enthusiasts. Blending tradition with technology, the SLK230 incorporates design elements of classic Mercedes sports cars like the 1950s' 300SL, and features the latest in safety technology—integrated roll-over bars, door-mounted side airbags, ASR traction control, and anti-lock brakes. *MBNA*

Petri, member of the Board of Management of Mercedes-Benz AG responsible for car development.

The SLK is designed to deliver an unrivaled driving experience 52 weeks a year. The long hood, wide doors, low windshield, and a dynamic rear end are key styling cues from the legendary roadster heritage combined with a contemporary design flair. Yet at the same time, the SLK redefines the concept of the sports car with sculptured side skirts and a "suit your fancy" all-new Vario roof.

Like its bigger brothers, the SLK230 has a fully automatic convertible top. But in the SLK230, that top is hard rather than cloth, as in the SLs. Pushing just one button initiates a sequence of events that begins with lowering the front and rear side windows. The roof is unlocked, the trunk is raised, the roof is opened, and the two-piece cover behind the roll bars is raised. The trunk lid is closed, and the front and rear side windows close. The entire procedure takes only 25 seconds.

Power for the SLK230 comes from a supercharged, 2.3-liter, inline four-cylinder engine producing 191 horsepower. This represents Mercedes-Benz's first postwar use of a supercharger in a production automobile. *MBNA*

A retractable luggage cover in the trunk must be in position before the Vario roof is operable. The cover prevents the roof from hitting stored items. Having the roof folded into the trunk, while still having a functional trunk lid, required some ingenuity. Other retractable hardtop-convertibles, such as the

To appeal to a younger market, the SLK230 has bright interior colors and ergonomically designed seats and instrument locations. Safety features include dual airbags in the dash and door-mounted side airbags, as well as side impact beams in the doors. *MBNA*

Ford Sunliner of the 1950s and the new Mitsubishi 3000GT VR-4 Spyder, do not possess this feature. The trunk lid opens backward to accommodate the folding roof. When the roof is stored and the trunk lid closes again, the trunk lid engages its forward hinges and can then be opened from the rear.

A unique draft stop distributes the air evenly throughout the interior evenly. It stretches over the roll-over bars with a few simple movements. "The front screen is designed to create maximum flowing contours together with the roof when it is up," explained Sacco. "The slope is a little more pronounced than on the SL, but it protects the passengers better from drafts."

No need to worry about storage space with the Vario roof. With the roof up, the SLK has up to 12.3 cubic feet of cargo in the trunk. With the roof lowered, about half the space remains available.

But beyond the trunk, the SLK sports very versatile carrying capabilities especially for sports equipment, accommodating the needs of young drivers and the young-at-heart. What's more impressive is that the roof rack may be used with the Vario roof open or closed. The SLK becomes a highly adaptable partner for leisure activities, sports, and hobbies with the availability of a variety of carrier systems.

The basic carrier consists of two side tubes which precisely match the shape of the Vario roof. These tubes function as a railing. Two aluminum cross struts provide additional stability and also serve to hold various racks. So whether its a snowboard, skis, surfboard, bicycle, boat, or luggage, there is a rack system equally as practical as those offered with other models.

In the past, design has been fairly conservative throughout Mercedes-Benz. But the SLK pushes these boundaries into the future with style and emotion. "It is indeed true that starting with the E-Class we began to underscore the emotional qualities of the individual model series, which in the future will lead to a greater variety of shapes and forms in the Mercedes-Benz vehicle range," said Sacco. "Most of the attributes which go to make a car have reached an international standard. Today, therefore, it is more important than ever to use design as a means of conveying image and prestige."

The SLK's design is a subtle blend of traditional and modern. The expressive face of the marque reflecting its style and identity, unmistakably identifies the SLK as a Mercedes-Benz.

"The small sports car is a new milestone in the new Mercedes-Benz passenger car product policy," said Helmut Werner, president and CEO of

Cutaway drawing of the SLK230 reveals the principal features of Mercedes-Benz's latest addition to its classic sports car line. The car's compact dimensions are evident, even without another car to compare it to. But also revealed are the 2.3-liter, supercharged, four-cylinder engine; the roll bars behind the driver and passenger; the independent front suspension; the five-link rear suspension; and the four-wheel disc brakes. *MBNA*

Mercedes-Benz AG. "This began with the new E-Class and is reaching unprecedented intensity this year with the launch of four new models. The SLK is a car which honors, in a particularly attractive form, our company's claim to offer premium value, and marks an aesthetic renaissance in automotive styling. More than this, with its lightness and flexibility, the SLK is in many ways symbolic of our company as a whole, which has become much faster-moving in recent years."

Just as the retracting soft top was a major feature of the R129 cars, a retracting hardtop was to be a feature of the SLK from its inception. Therefore, the stylists had the challenge of making the car act and look like a coupe with the roof raised. Some retractable hardtops look ungainly with the roof raised and Mercedes-Benz didn't want this on the SLK. At the same time, the designers had to obtain the look of a classic roadster with the top down, with no part of its structure showing. This is a feature of

the R129 tops, while, for example, the retracted top of the Jaguar XK8 is raised slightly above the rear deck.

"We developed a perfectly functioning technical solution [to the top]," said Sacco. "The design and marketing sectors then took pleasure in integrating it into the SLK."

This achievement was quite a challenge for the Mercedes-Benz design team. "The greatest difficulty in developing the design of the SLK was certainly to ensure that the contours of all the joints were harmonious in spite of the exceptional sequence of movements of the roof, and the space which it requires," added Sacco.

With a relatively long wheelbase and short overhangs at the front and rear, the SLK gains maximum interior space from the package while giving it a sleek appearance. The taillights are integrated well into the rear-end design. Inspiration for the taillight design on the SLK came from the C-Class. The red-gray color of the wraparound lenses and

With the top up or down, the SLK230 is a smooth design and worthy of inclusion in the revered Mercedes-Benz SL line that stretches back to the original 300SL. *MBNA*

built-in "resonator," which works like the security tags sometimes attached to merchandise in retail stores.

A low-power electronic signal from the car prompts a return signal from the resonator in the infant seat, allowing the system to sense the presence of the seat and automatically turn off the passenger-side airbag. The seat requires no battery or power hookup, since the signal from the car is reflected back by the resonator in the infant seat. A light on the center console confirms "airbag off."

Development costs for the SLK were about $330 million. The total capital needed, including investment, launch, and sales added up to approximately $650 million. About $200 million was invested at the Bremen plant where the SLK and the bigger, more expensive SL roadster are produced.

The 1998 SLK went on sale in the United States in February 1997 with a price close to $40,000 driven by the market and competition. One goal is to capture new and younger customers for Mercedes-Benz. The median age of 30–39 is expected to attract equal numbers of men and women with an annual household income of $80,000. Loyal Mercedes-Benz owners drawn to the exclusive appeal of a limited-availability model may purchase an SLK as an additional vehicle.

The SLK goes head-to-head with the successful BMW Z3, focusing on performance and image and costing $10,000 less. Soon after the SLK, the Porsche Boxster made its debut, expecting to draw on Porsche's sports car heritage and emphasize performance, in a more affordable, style than the 911.

The United States is expected to receive 15 percent of annual SLK production, or approximately 6,000 out of 35,000 units in 1997. The United States will be the largest export market for the SLK.

MUSEUMS

Stuttgart

Mercedes-Benz is both fortunate and prescient. The company had the foresight many years ago to preserve important vehicles in its history, and it continues to use the Mercedes-Benz Museum in Stuttgart-Unterturkheim as a valuable resource. Lovers of Mercedes-Benz cars, and the cars of the two companies that preceded them, are fortunate to have this kind of resource for researching restorations or simply for enjoyment on a trip to Germany. Few other museums of the world, with the possible exception of the Henry Ford Museum and Greenfield Village in Dearborn, Michigan, have such a complete collection of their sponsors' products, and equally few maintain these vehicles in such pristine and operable condition.

As William Stobbs wrote in *Motor Museums of Europe*: "The museum is almost unparalleled in both the quality of the vehicles displayed, and the organization of the museum itself. The archives preserve the drawings, facts, and photographic material, and a well-informed staff explains (in five languages) the details of engineering for the cars and engines displayed."

Opened in 1961, the museum houses collections that were begun in the days of Gottlieb Daimler and Karl Benz. Many of these treasures were once stored in locked rooms, but since the end of World War II, they began to be shown more frequently to the public. Alfred Neubauer, head of Mercedes' racing programs before and after the war, was the catalyst behind the collection. More than 850,000 people visit the museum annually.

Most of the historic vehicles in the building were found and then restored to perfection in every detail. Since 1971, though, Mercedes has withdrawn models from production for inclusion in the museum's collection. Vehicles are rotated from storage and may travel to exhibits and international motoring events around the world.

Tuscaloosa/Vance, Alabama

In the new Mercedes-Benz USI All-Activity Vehicle (M-Type) assembly facility in Vance, Alabama, near Tuscaloosa, Mercedes-Benz will have not only a Visitor Center, which will lead visitors through Mercedes' long and glorious history, but also a small museum, with some significant Mercedes-Benz vehicles included. At the time of this writing, the final contents had not been determined. While the total vehicle count cannot approach that of Stuttgart, the Visitor Center and museum will allow American visitors at least a glimpse of Mercedes' heritage.

APPENDIX B
CLUBS

Gullwing Group International

The Gullwing Group International was founded in 1961 "for those interested in the maintenance and preservation of the Mercedes-Benz 300SL Coupe and Roadster." As of 1995, the club had 690 members. There is an annual convention (in 1996 it was in Portland, Oregon), and the group publishes the *300 Starletter* monthly newsletter for its members. Annual dues are $55 in the United States and $75 for those outside the United States. For additional information, contact Barbara Hunt, P.O. Box 1569, Morgan Hill, CA 95038-1569, Telephone: (408) 776-7488.

Mercedes-Benz 190SL Group

This is a smaller organization devoted to the preservation and dissemination of information concerning the 190SL. For additional information, contact David Rosales, 16 Theodore Dr., East Brunswick, NJ 08816. Telephone: (908) 651-1033.

Mercedes-Benz Club of America

The largest Mercedes-Benz club in the world is the Mercedes-Benz Club of America, with over 23,000 members. Founded in 1956, the club publishes the excellent *The Star* magazine six times a year. Its aim is to organize events for Mercedes-Benz owners that stress technical topics, driving events, and social activity. Members are assigned to the nearest local section. Dues are $35 a year in the U. S., $45 elsewhere. The annual convention is "StarFest," which in 1996 was held in Portland, Oregon. "StarTech 97," the club's biannual technical weekend brings together dozens of experts for maintenance and restoration seminars. For additional information about the club, contact Ron Farrar, Executive Director, MBCA, 1907 Lelaray Street, Colorado Springs, CO 80909. Telephone: 800-637-2360.

APPENDIX C
BIBLIOGRAPHY

Adler, Dennis. *Mercedes-Benz: 110 Years of Excellence.* Motorbooks International, 1995.

Alfredi, Bruno. *Mercedes-Benz 300SL, 300SL-24, 500SL.* Automobilia, 1989.

Barrett, Frank. *Illustrated Mercedes-Benz Buyer's Guide.* Motorbooks International, 1994.

Clarke, R.M. *Mercedes-Benz 230/250/280SL 1963–1971.* Brooklands Books.

Clarke, R.M. *Mercedes 350/450SL & SLC 1971–1980.* Brooklands Books.

Cutter, Robert, and Bob Fendell. *Encyclopedia of Auto Racing Greats.* Prentice-Hall, 1973.

Kimes, Beverly Rae. *The Star and the Laurel: The Centennial History of Daimler, Mercedes and Benz.* Mercedes-Benz of North America, 1986.

Laban, Brian. *Mercedes SL Series: The Complete Story.* Crowood Autoclassics Series, 1992.

Langworth, Richard M. *Mercedes-Benz: The First Hundred Years.* Consumer Guide Classic Car Series, 1984.

Ludvigsen, Karl. *Mercedes-Benz Quicksilver Century.* Transport Bookman Publications, 1995.

Nallinger, Fritz, Prof. Dr. Ing. e.h. *Gottlieb Daimler and Karl Benz.* Special Edition from Die Grossen Deutschen, Daimler-Benz AG, 1967.

Neubauer, Alfred. *Speed Was My Life.* Clarkson N. Potter, Inc., 1958.

Niemann, Dr. Harry. *Béla Barényi: The Father of Passive Safety.* Mercedes-Benz AG, 1994.

Nitske, W. Robert. *Mercedes-Benz Production Models Book: 1946–1995.* Motorbooks International, 1995.

Sacco, Bruno. *Mercedes-Benz Design.* Mercedes-Benz of North America, 1988.

Setright, L.J.K. *Mercedes-Benz SL & SLC.* Osprey Publishing, Ltd., 1986.

Taylor, James. *The Mercedes-Benz Since 1945.* Motor Racing Publications, Ltd., 1985.

INDEX